LONG AND SHORT

Long and Short

72 Stories by Groww to Unravel Stock Markets

Groww

BLOOMSBURY
NEW DELHI • LONDON • OXFORD • NEW YORK • SYDNEY

BLOOMSBURY INDIA
Bloomsbury Publishing India Pvt. Ltd
Second Floor, LSC Building No. 4, DDA Complex, Pocket C – 6 & 7,
Vasant Kunj, New Delhi, 110070

BLOOMSBURY, BLOOMSBURY INDIA and the Diana logo
are trademarks of Bloomsbury Publishing Plc

First published in 2025
This edition published 2025

Copyright © Billionbrains Garage Ventures Private Limited, 2025

Artwork created by Design101 Studio LLP for Groww

Groww has asserted its right under the Indian Copyright Act
to be identified as the Author of this work

All rights reserved. No part of this publication may be reproduced or transmitted in any form or by any means, electronic or mechanical, including photocopying, recording or any information storage or retrieval system, without prior permission in writing from the publishers

This book is solely the responsibility of the author and the publisher has had no role in the creation of the content and does not have responsibility for anything defamatory or libellous or objectionable

Bloomsbury Publishing Plc does not have any control over, or responsibility for, any third-party websites referred to or in this book. All internet addresses given in this book were correct at the time of going to press. The author and publisher regret any inconvenience caused if addresses have changed or sites have ceased to exist but can accept no responsibility for any such changes

Investments in securities market are subject to market risks, read all the related documents carefully before investing. The securities are quoted as an example and not as a recommendation

For more information, visit: https://groww.in/p/disclosure

ISBN: PB: 978-93-61318-90-0; eBook: 978-93-61312-66-3

2 4 6 8 10 9 7 5 3 1

Typeset in Bembo by Manipal Technologies Limited
Printed and bound in India by Thomson Press India Ltd

To find out more about our authors and books visit www.bloomsbury.com and sign up for our newsletters

Contents

A Note from the CEO viii

1. Explaining What Is Already Known 1
2. Don't Always Chase the Best 4
3. Leverage Cuts Both Ways 7
4. How 2020 Moved the Markets 10
5. The Right Way to Make Money 14
6. Investments That Kill 17
7. Investing in the Unknown 19
8. Everyone Knows This Brand 23
9. It's Small Folk Versus the Big Fish 26
10. Every Single Star 29
11. Investments With and Without Upper Limit ... 32
12. Stick to What Suits You 35
13. When Does a Bubble Pop? 39
14. The Thin Line Between Crazy Good and Just Crazy 42
15. Formula to Hold the Best Performers 44
16. The Missing Link That Negates All Else 47
17. How Many Winners Can There Be? 50
18. Some Winners Keep Winning 53
19. What Changed While You Were Looking at the Stock Price 56
20. How One of the Greatest Authors in History Invested His Money 59
21. Where Does Your Advisor Invest? 62
22. The Man Who Gives the Most 65
23. Chase the Life and Not the Lifestyle 67

24	Korean Shipbuilding	71
25	Why Do Stocks Go Up?	74
26	What Are Others Doing?	77
27	If Not This, Then That	80
28	Which Strategy You Adopt	84
29	Look Left and Right to Cross the Road	88
30	Only Correct Information Is Useful	92
31	Whom Not to Take Advice From	96
32	What Happened in 2008	102
33	IPO Frenzy of the Late 1990s	105
34	The Lesser-Known Tulip Tale	107
35	Which Game Are You Playing?	110
36	The Risk Nobody Prepared For	113
37	How Does It Scale?	118
38	The Monday Unlike Any Other	121
39	Bad Decisions and Good Outcomes	124
40	Yes, They Will Fall Someday!	127
41	Remember This the Next Time You Hear a Dire Prediction	130
42	Not Keeping All Your Eggs in One Basket Isn't Enough	133
43	How Much Does a 2BHK in Rural China Affect You?	137
44	The Unheard-of Investor Known for Speed	140
45	High Returns, but Much Higher Risk	143
46	More Information Isn't Always Better	146
47	Simple Is Not Easy	150
48	The Most Quoted Trader of All Time	154
49	The Deepest Recession	158
50	What Happened in 1992?	162
51	Journey from Start to IPO and Beyond	166
52	The Advice That Didn't Work in Japan	171
53	Rules That Stopped Making Sense	174
54	The J-Curve of Internet Companies	178
55	Is It a Pond or Is It an Ocean?	182

56	All That 2021 Was	186
57	Why Does Gold Have Value?	191
58	Avoid the Big Losses	194
59	Evolve or Die	197
60	Are You Reading Through Your IPO?	201
61	Factory of the World	204
62	When Geniuses Got Together	208
63	How Did It Start?	211
64	What Happened in 1991?	215
65	Making No Mistakes	219
66	Markets and Wars	223
67	Asian Fish in American Waters	226
68	How Does Russia's War Affect Petrol?	230
69	When Your Gain Is Someone's Loss	234
70	The (Dis)Advantages of Being Big	237
71	Investments Beyond Numbers	240
72	Just Keep Investing?	244

Notes	247
About the Author	255

A Note from the CEO

In 2016, when Groww was still in its early stages, we launched a newsletter. The newsletter was primarily a collection of noteworthy articles curated from across the internet. As Groww developed, the newsletter evolved into what we now call 'Groww Digest'. Over the years, 'Groww Digest' underwent several transformations, from curating external content to writing original pieces. Throughout these changes, one aspect remained consistent: our intention to help readers enhance their knowledge. Today, our audience has grown to over 1.5 crore. 'Groww Digest' is intentionally free of any product-related information; it is not about updates, features or launches. Instead, it focuses on learning and the investor.

In this book, we present the first seventy-two stories from our weekly 'Groww Digest' series. We have observed that our readers learn about finances better when stories from the real world resonate with them. 'Groww Digest' emails are exclusively for Groww customers. This book will give a wider readership access to a curated selection of these stories.

Lalit Keshre

1

Explaining What Is Already Known

A FEW YEARS AGO, THERE was a car that meant a lot to a company. Let's just call it Car-X. It wasn't selling well. This was a problem. The company decided to do something about it. Engineers were asked to make the car perfect. And they got to work. It reached a point where it wasn't just office work for the engineers. They were emotionally invested in the car.

Some engineers took to social media to express how proud they were of the work they had done on it. Not just the engineers, even the executives left no stone unturned. They gave the car four or five variants. The lowest variant barely had any features. But it was cheap. The highest variant had all the bells and whistles — alloy wheels, airbags, leather seats — you name it.

FIGURE 1.1 Engineers working on a car model

And then, for the engine options, they went all out. For people with a small budget, there was a small petrol engine. For people who drove a lot, there was an efficient diesel engine. For the enthusiastic types, there was a powerful engine. And each of these engines came in many variants. So, this one car, Car-X, had around fifteen different versions.

The company wanted this to be a car for every kind of customer. The car was launched. It sold. Did it sell as well as the company hoped? No. Not even close. In some small circles of car enthusiasts and automotive journalists, the discussion started. What went wrong? Gradually, a certain opinion became more popular than others. The opinion was that Car-X had too many variants.

FIGURE 1.2 Board meeting about Car-X and its variants

How is a customer supposed to choose which one to buy? 'Cognitive overload'. A lack of clear identity for the car. Here's a question: these people who were so certain the car didn't do well because of the number of versions – why didn't they say the same when the car was first launched? Why did they wait for the car to underperform?

The answer is simple: it's easy to tell a story when you know the ending. This is called hindsight bias. It affects us all. We feel we knew something all along. This makes us confident. Even though we didn't actually know how things would turn out, we end up believing we did. And then we assume that we would be able to predict future events.

Can you imagine how this would play out while investing? Today Sensex is above 45,000. And this very Sensex was at 26,000 – not even ten months ago! And to many, the recovery of the markets seems obvious! 'This had to happen.' Somehow, everyone is quick to explain how the markets got here. Ask them to explain where the markets will be ten months from now.

Most will not have a clue. And some will make predictions, sure. But their track record of being right is abysmal. Most things in real life operate under such complex situations, nobody can predict them. It is best to not fall for fancy explanations from the past. And just because there is an explanation of the past, doesn't mean the explanation is correct.

The manufacturer of Car-X launched other new cars. They improved many things besides the cars, including its service, marketing, dealer network and so on. Today, some of their other cars sell in very high volumes. They've become tough competition – the stuff of nightmares for their competitors. And yes, they still offer many different variants and engines.

2

Don't Always Chase the Best

Depending on where you are, betting on sports may be legal or illegal. But it happens all over the world. One such sport is the 100-metre sprint. All 100-metre races are extremely tight. Choosing whom to put your money on is so difficult, it appears more to be about luck than about looking at the athletes' training regimes.

The winners are not separated by seconds. They're separated by fractions of a second. The difference between the first and the second is often less than 0.1 seconds. That's 100 milliseconds. When you blink, your eyes are shut for around 100 milliseconds. That is how tight 100-metre races are.

FIGURE 2.1 A 100-metre race in the Beijing Olympics

Don't Always Chase the Best

If you conduct a race among the best athletes of a high school or college, you might get a few who can run the race in under 12 seconds. But you will struggle to find someone who can finish it in under 11 seconds. Walter Dix was no regular person. He finished a 100-metre race in 10.28 seconds while in his final year of high school. He's from the US and by the time he was in college, he was shattering records held in national-level sports.

In 2008, he ran in the 100-metre race in the Beijing Olympics and competed against Richard Thompson. Richard Thompson is so blisteringly fast; he is called Richard 'Torpedo' Thompson. He's from Trinidad and Tobago – an island country in the Atlantic Ocean – just beside Venezuela in South America. Richard too has many medals to his name.

Both these athletes are top-notch. Both have lots of medals. Both have set blistering record times. Before going to Beijing, these were the best times reported by the athletes – Walter Dix: 10.06 seconds; Richard Thompson: 10.44 seconds. And when these two were in Beijing, they absolutely shattered their own records! But who won? Richard beat Walter Dix.

Walter Dix: 9.91 seconds. Richard Thompson: 9.89 seconds. Yes, that's the difference – 0.02 seconds. One-fifth of the time it takes to blink your eyes. On the day the race was conducted, can you imagine how these athletes would be feeling? Waking up early morning, mentally preparing, possibly exercising and meditating?

There was another athlete who, according to reports, woke up, ate some chicken nuggets, watched some TV, slept again and then went racing in the same 100-metre race. At the end of the race, this athlete's foot was photographed with his shoelaces undone in an Olympic race. With just that description, it would appear that this chicken-nugget-eating athlete stood no chance at winning.

This athlete too shattered his own record. In fact, he shattered his own and every other record at that time. He came first. Gold medal. His name is Usain Bolt. Usain Bolt: 9.69 seconds. Walter Dix: 9.89 seconds. Richard Thompson: 9.91 seconds. If you were betting, choosing which person would come first or second or third would be extremely tough, to say the least.

If you put your money on the athlete who came fourth, you would lose your money. Unfortunately, many think investing is similar. And thankfully, it isn't. Yes, knowing which athlete or stock or mutual fund will perform best is impossibly challenging even if you have all the information in the world.

But unlike betting on athletes, in investing, you don't need to choose the best stock or mutual fund! If you choose the first, you'll make a lot of money. If you choose the second, you'll make a lot of money – a bit less, but still a lot. Third – you'll still make money. Fourth – still yes. And that goes on for the fifth, sixth and so on.

The best-performing stock or mutual fund keeps changing from time to time. If you keep changing stocks and mutual funds to always run after the one performing the best, you'll end up paying a lot of fees and taxes and not getting much else in return. Investing isn't betting on one in ten best athletes. Investing is kind of like betting on many good athletes.

3

Leverage Cuts Both Ways

We've all heard about this. Leverage allows us to do more. You can't carry 500 kilograms. But with wheels, you can drag that much. That's leverage. In finance speak, the more money you have, the more you can make – if (and that is a very big 'if') you do it right. Companies and individuals take loans or funding to do much more than they could otherwise.

Some of the biggest names today – Apple, Google, Facebook and Amazon – none of them would exist had it not been for the financial leverage they got in the form of funding in their initial years. And just like several others, Boeing and Airbus took loans. In 1969, Boeing bought out a stellar aircraft: the Boeing 747. You have almost certainly seen it. It is a double-decker towards the front of the aircraft.

It can carry more than 600 passengers and is a very popular aircraft. In 1990, a group of European companies started working on a competitor to the Boeing 747. In 2000, these companies formed what is now known as Airbus. After nearly fifteen years of development, Airbus displayed to the world what was an impossible sight. The Airbus A380 – the world's largest passenger plane.

It could carry more than 800 passengers (nearly as much as a train can). It was a proper double-decker – front to back. It had 50 per cent more floor space than the Boeing 747.

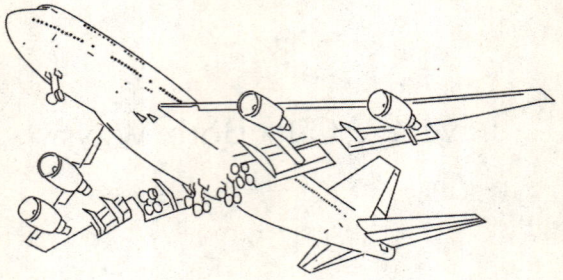

FIGURE 3.1 World's largest passenger plane – Airbus A380

In 2005, this giant took to the skies for the first time. Nobody could believe the plane could climb and turn at the angles it did. They even intentionally scraped the tail of the plane while taking off to show how resilient it was.

Orders started flowing in. Of course, Airbus took a massive loan to develop this aircraft. On the other side of the Atlantic Ocean, in the US, Boeing had also taken loans. But they weren't working on an even larger aircraft. They were working on this: the Boeing 787 Dreamliner – a relatively small aircraft that would be more efficient. This would seat only around 250 people.

They were betting that smaller, more efficient planes would be the future. Without the loans, the companies wouldn't have been able to embark on these missions. The idea was that the leverage provided by the loans would allow them to make a product so good that their profits would swell, and with that, they would easily be able to pay back the loans.

The jumbo plane, Airbus A380, got all the attention you would expect. Thankfully for Airbus and Boeing, the orders started coming in. And they kept paying back their loans. A few years later, things turned out differently than some had thought. Yes, more people were flying, but they were flying to newer, smaller destinations in smaller numbers. It just wasn't that more people were flying on the same route.

To fly at a profit, airlines need to fill a minimum number of seats in a plane. On the Boeing 787, it was easier. On the Airbus A380, it was much harder. Orders for the Airbus A380 started drying up. The Boeing 787 was doing fine. At this stage, the leverage provided by the giant loans started cutting the other way for Airbus. They had to pay back but didn't have the profits they thought they would from the Airbus A380.

Airbus finally decided to pull the plug. No more Airbus A380. Paying back the loan has become a giant headache for Airbus. Thankfully for Airbus, it has a couple of other planes that sell very well. If you've flown on an Indigo Airlines plane, you were probably on this super successful Airbus plane. Maybe if they had been too ambitious and taken an outsized loan, they would be in much deeper trouble.

And Boeing – while Boeing's 787 is selling well – has run into some big issues with another aircraft. Unfortunately, the issue pertains to its highest-selling aircraft. Two Boeing 737-MAX planes have crashed and the blame for that is falling on poor quality control. So yes, even Boeing has issues with loans. Reliance had to take massive loans. Billions of dollars.

Without that, none of India's smartphone revolutions would have come to be. Thankfully for Reliance, with Jio, it created a money-printing behemoth. It was able to service its loans just fine. This year, however, they went a step ahead. It raised enough money to pay back all its loans. All $21 billion of it. Reliance did leverage right.

4

How 2020 Moved the Markets

2020 HAS BEEN ... THE year started with some scares – but that, in hindsight, happens all the time.

- 27 December 2019: Sensex was at 41,575. Exactly a year ago.
- 3 January 2020: Sensex closed at 41,464. The US kills Iran's key military leader. Third World War scare spreads across the globe.[1]
- 9 January 2020: Sensex was at 41,452. WHO recognises the existence of a virus in China. World markets remain unaffected.
- 14 January 2020: Sensex closed at 41,952. Indian markets hit a new all-time high.
- 22 January 2020: Sensex was at 41,115. First records of cases affected by the virus emerge. There are 607 cases as of this date.
- 30 January 2020: Sensex closed at 40,913. The first cases of the virus were detected in India among students returning from China. In China, the total were detected cases are 9,865.[2]
- 3 February 2020: Sensex was at 39,872. Union budget in India is announced.
- 19 February 2020: Sensex was was at 41,323. The virus starts being detected across the globe. Italy and Iran report high numbers. Markets start a downward trend. Total cases recorded are 76,103.

- 6 March 2020: Sensex closed at 37,567. Markets' downtrend catches speed. A banking crisis unfolds. The next few days see some of the biggest single-day market falls ever. Total cases in the world: 1,09,587.
- 12 March 2020: Sensex was at 32,778. WHO declares the situation to be a pandemic.
- 23 March 2020: Sensex closed at 25,981. The world's highest single-day fall is observed. Sensex is down over 13 per cent in a single day. A day later, India goes into lockdown. The lockdowns were meant to last three weeks but were extended a few more times in the following weeks.
- 20 April 2020: Sensex was at 31,648. West Texas Intermediate (WTI) crude oil price goes negative.
- 23 April 2020: Sensex closed at 31,863. Franklin Templeton India debt fund crisis unfolds. Six debt funds are wound down.
- 26 May 2020: Sensex shut at 30,609. Domestic flights restart in India.
- 30 June 2020: Sensex closed at 34,915. Indian company Bharat Biotech announces India-made vaccine and starts phase 1 trials in July. At the same time, Moderna, Pfizer and AstraZeneca reach advanced stages of trials with their own vaccines. Over the next months, vaccines by Moderna, Pfizer and AstraZeneca clear hurdle after hurdle.
- 16 September 2020: Sensex was at 39,302. India experiences the highest number of cases in a single day – over 97,000 cases. This marked the peak. After this, daily cases kept declining.[3]
- 4 November 2020: Sensex closed at 40,616. US election exit polls start coming in. After a nail-biting few days, it becomes clear that Joe Biden is going to be the next president of the US.

- 9 November 2020: Sensex closed at 42,597. Sensex touches a new all-time high surpassing the high touched on 14 January 2020.
- 1 December 2020: Sensex was at 44,655. Moderna announces an efficacy rate for its vaccine – 94.5 per cent.[4]
- 9 December 2020: Sensex closed at 46,103. The UK becomes the first country to start administering vaccines to the public.
- 21 December 2020: Sensex was at 45,553. A new strain of the virus is detected in the UK. Markets fall 3 per cent. Vaccine companies claim the existing vaccines will be able to fight the new strain as well. Markets recover.
- 24 December 2020: Sensex was at 47,053. Markets touch a new all-time high.
- 27 December 2020: We're here today. Quite the ride.

Here are a few thoughts. Bear in mind, these are not what we are saying is right or wrong. They are just thoughts you can ponder over. Nobody truly knows. Nobody predicted the virus in December 2019. Nobody also predicted that the markets would recover so fast in April 2020. The Centres for Disease Control and Prevention (CDC) asked citizens to not buy N95 masks earlier. WHO initially said there was no need to shut down international flights.

Volatility is a non-event. If the markets went down and then came back up, does it matter that they went down in between? Sensex one-year returns we see that: returns at the end of 2016 are 11 per cent, returns at the end of 2017 are 30 per cent, at the end of 2018 are 0.8 per cent, at the end of 2019 are 12 per cent and returns at the end of 2020 are 15 per cent.

One of these years saw a globe-shutting pandemic. Looking at just the returns, which year was it? Risk and margin of safety. In 2019, many thought the next recession would be caused by an inverting yield curve. Others thought a Third World War would be a reason. And then an invisible virus got on several international flights and caused great damage internationally.

No matter the reason for the trouble, a margin of safety was the saviour. Emergency money or safe investments, whatever you call it, saves the day when it comes to unseen risks. Nothing is truly safe. Even people investing in bank's Fixed Deposit (FD) in recent years have suffered. Every investment is a risky one – it's just a matter of how risky. Makes sense to plan accordingly.

This isn't the first virus we've heard of since 1918. In just the last two decades, we've seen Severe Acute Respiratory Syndrome (SARS), bird flu, swine flu, Ebola, Nipah and a few others. It's impossible to say which one will become big. There's always going to be something to worry about. And unless you work in public health, there's little you can do except make sure you're prepared for tough times – whether they be viruses, bad weather, bad economic policies, international rifts or something else.

Long term. Nothing is permanent – true for economies, markets and rules of markets. But some things last longer than others. The one rule so many investors swear by – investing for the long term – was valid before the pandemic and is valid while we're in it and will likely be valid after the pandemic too.

Sensex twenty-year returns on 27 December 2019 were 11.37 per cent, whereas Sensex twenty-year returns on 27 December 2020 were 13.28 per cent.

5

The Right Way to Make Money

There was a young mechanic on the West Coast of the US. Let's call him Eric. He had worked on repairing various cars since he finished high school. After almost seven years of that, he became a father and decided to increase his income. He got himself a job at a used car dealership as a salesman. There, he saw the best salesman sell a car that had been in an accident to a single mother.

'No accidents, no mechanical failures. All good,' he told her. That salesman was rewarded with a hefty commission from that sale. So that's what needs to be done to sell cars: lie. But Eric couldn't do it. He quit his job and joined another dealership hoping they would be a bit more truthful with their customers.

Unfortunately, for him, that wasn't the case. 'This car has a turbo that makes funny noises but if you keep the customer engaged, he won't notice it. Hopefully, the turbo will go bad only after we've sold the car,' his boss once told him. 'Why can't we just repair the turbo?' he asked. 'We're a dealership. Not a garage,' was what he was told.

In the meantime, he bought himself a second-hand Volkswagen Jetta at a really cheap price from a friend he had known. The car had been in a flood and therefore it had electrical and mechanical damage. Things had been repaired but everything didn't work perfectly. Eric, being a mechanic, thought he would be able to maintain his car's repairs if something bothered him too much.

A couple of months later, when he changed his wiper motors after already having changed various other parts, he had had enough. In a salvage yard where cars written off by insurance companies were kept, he found a Volkswagen Jetta that had been in a crash. The body structure was smashed from the back. There was no hope of the car ever running again.

But its engine and electricals were fine. He bought this car for barely any money. Over a few weeks, he took out parts from the crashed car and fitted them into his own car. He ended up with a car that was completely healthy and free of problems and from there, his story unfolded as you would expect.

He was doing something others in his area weren't thinking of. Like them, he was selling older cars. But while other dealerships would try to buy good cars and sell them for a profit, he would buy two old cars with different flaws. And then he would try to interchange parts to make one good car.

There are several entrepreneurs like Eric who work on cars similarly. In fact, there are such people working similarly in the space of laptops, smartphones, appliances and watches.

Talking of other companies, how do you think Apple makes its money? Until 2007, when Steve Jobs walked on stage and introduced the world to the iPhone, Apple's main source of income was computers. It is now majorly iPhones.

What about McDonald's? This is a brand so famous for its burgers, there are actually places on Earth where people have heard of McDonald's but haven't heard of Santa Claus. How do they make money? Burgers, sure. Fries, yes. Real estate? A big yes.

McDonald's owns commercial space in areas so prime that even luxury watch brands struggle to find space.

They have space near Big Ben in London, Times Square in New York and Red Square in Moscow. They earn rent from these places and that keeps them afloat when burgers aren't selling well enough.

Shell, the petrol pump company, also sells groceries and coffee. PVR is famous for movies and popcorn. There was a firm that used machine learning and artificial intelligence to analyse the live speeches of politicians as they made important announcements. A few seconds before the news was announced, they'd be able to make a guess about the news being good or bad based on the tone of the voice. They'd make bets in the markets and earn money in just those few seconds.

What's common between all of these companies? They all make money. Apple makes money in ways you expect it to. McDonald's makes money in a way not many expect it to. But they all make money. And that's the thing about investing. There's no right or wrong. If it makes money for you, it's right for you.

6

Investments That Kill

Heard of Kodak, the photography company? Or the film reels used in cameras? Kodak absolutely dominated that space. The brand was the fifth most valuable in the world. The Apple iPhone sold 50 per cent of all phones in the US. Maruti Suzuki sold 50 per cent of all cars in India.[1] Kodak sold 66 per cent of all film reels in the world.

The second-largest company after Kodak was so small that barely anybody had heard of them. Then, someone invented the digital camera. You know what happened after that. But here's something not many know: the first digital camera prototype was made by an engineer named Steve Sasson and he worked at … Kodak. Kodak did try to do something with it but failed to capitalise on this early move. That's not the only ship Kodak missed. In 2001, before Facebook or Instagram were born, Kodak acquired a photo-sharing startup called Ofoto.

Today, for many, it is hard to imagine a world without picture-sharing platforms like Instagram. Kodak had it in 2001. Kodak tried to use that company to make more people print pictures. In 2012, Kodak filed for bankruptcy. Kodak does not dominate the way it once did. While earlier, practically everybody had heard of it, today, not many remember. This isn't to say Kodak wasn't good at making decisions. What appear to be poor decisions now seem so only because we know what happened. This is hindsight bias.

A mistake (almost) killed Kodak. And everyone makes mistakes. As investors too, we cannot avoid making mistakes. They will happen. The most successful organisations and people have a closet of skeletons – mistakes.

Mistakes are the fuel of success. You make a thousand attempts, one succeeds. Apple Newton. Never heard of it? This is because it failed; it was a smartphone. Zune, Microsoft's competitor to the iPod, also failed. Tesla's Roadster, an electric vehicle, also failed. Amazon Fire Phone too was not able to leave a lasting impact.

The list of failed items is probably longer than those that succeeded. Not all of your investments will give you solid returns. There will be bad ones. There will be promising ones that never took off. There will be those that did extremely well but crashed right before you could take advantage of it. What we can do is ensure that when a mistake does happen, it doesn't kill us. Survivability comes first. And that survivability comes from diversification.

The Apple iPhone practically killed BlackBerry and Nokia. But they couldn't kill Samsung. BlackBerry and Nokia made phones. Samsung made phones among other things. When investing, the priority is to survive. If you lose all your money today and a new opportunity comes up tomorrow, how will you take advantage of it?

7

Investing in the Unknown

AMAZON KNOWS ONE THING well: selling things online. Yes, there are other things too but its expertise in selling online is something very few would dispute. Amazon has a presence in the US, Canada, India, Japan, Brazil, several European countries, the UAE and a few other countries. Around 38 per cent of all e-commerce sales in the US are dominated by Amazon. The next big player is Walmart with around 6 per cent market share. In the UK, Amazon has about 30 per cent. Next is eBay with only around 10 per cent. See the difference between the first and the second?

In India, Flipkart rules but by a very slim margin. Both Flipkart and Amazon have about 31 per cent. That's what Amazon does: sell online. There's a concept in investing that Warren Buffett and Charlie Munger both speak about: the circle of competence.[1] Stick to what you know. Warren Buffett has stayed away from technology stocks, saying he doesn't understand them. He understands insurance. He understands the railroad. So that's where he mainly invests.

Amazon was born in the US and has developed its expertise on certain logistical foundations that the US offers – good roads, good internet, an English-speaking population and large warehouses. These are logistics that are not found in many parts of Africa. This is why Amazon doesn't have much of a presence on the continent.[2]

As a continent, Africa is extremely diverse, lacks infrastructure in many places, accessibility remains an issue, internet penetration is increasing but is very patchy, residential addresses aren't clearly defined – and that's just mentioning a few of the issues.[3] Jumia – an e-commerce startup that began in 2012 – is known as the 'Amazon of Africa'.

Starting with Nigeria, Jumia has expanded to other African countries like Egypt, Morocco and South Africa. Jumia built its own logistics network in Africa. Its website and application are optimised to function at low internet speeds. Jumia has designated pick-up spots in neighbourhoods. Jumia understands e-commerce. So does Amazon. Jumia understands Africa. Amazon doesn't. Maybe that's why Amazon hasn't tried too hard to enter Africa.

FIGURE 7.1 Delivery person delivering food to a woman

In recent times, there has been a content boom on the internet. Pictures, videos and texts of all kinds have flooded everybody's handheld devices. We're a part of that revolution too. In a certain part of the internet, where people love to learn and discuss finance, 'circle of competence' has become a phrase that's much repeated, and rightly so.

A message that's half transmitted is as good as no message. While many are busy talking about sticking to one's own circle of competence, a certain part of Buffett's message often gets ignored: expand your circle of competence. Nobody is born with a set of competencies. They are learned and developed over time.

So why stop after learning a few things? In a world that's rapidly changing, not expanding your circle of competence can prove to be a deadly mistake. For over sixty years that Warren Buffett has been an active investor, he has mostly stayed away from technology stocks. In 2016, at the age of eighty-five, he made a big investment in technology. He bought Apple stocks – something which was once outside his circle of competence. At the time, Apple stock comprised 5.8 per cent of his total investments. In 2022, Apple stocks were the biggest of his investments by value. That 5.8 per cent has grown to 48 per cent of all of his investments.

Amazon sticks to its circle of competence. But it also explores beyond it. Sometimes it does well, sometimes it does not. In fact, if all companies did was stick to their circle of competence without ever expanding, they'd die. Netflix, the streaming service, was in the business of renting DVDs. Then it moved to online streaming. Now, Netflix is a verb. Similarly, Reliance's core competence was polyester, then it became oil. Now it is communication, and it's now trying its hand at retail.

Nokia was a paper mill company. Then, it was unbeatable in mobile technology. They couldn't expand their competence after that. Tata was a trading company. You are aware of all that it does. Google was known for its search engine. Now it is also known for most of the smartphones on Earth. Coca-Cola makes soda and cola. They're also becoming a major maker of health drinks. In investing too, things change. Sticking to what you already know may work for you for a very short duration or for your lifetime. Nobody can tell. Keep learning!

8

Everyone Knows This Brand

HAVE YOU HAD Coca-Cola? There's no point asking this question, we know you have. Coca-Cola has become one of the most recognisable brands in the world today. No matter which part of the world you go to, you will almost certainly be able to find a banner with the Coca-Cola logo on it.

The Coca-Cola we're drinking now has been around since the early 1900s.[1] It still tastes the same, looks the same and is named the same. And somehow, it still hasn't stopped being 'cool'. Around 1.7 billion servings of Coca-Cola are served every day (the population of the world is around 8.2 billion).

What's the most understood English word in the world? It is 'okay' followed by Coca-Cola. Can you name a product that is cool now and was also cool in the 1930s? There are very few. There have been competitors: Mountain Dew, Red Bull, Fanta, Thums Up and Pepsi, to name a few. None were able to dethrone Coca-Cola.

The Coca-Cola product in itself isn't particularly anything to write home about. It's mostly sugary soda water. And yet, it is sold in more than 200 countries. The company spends around $4 billion on advertisement and marketing. Apple spends 'only' about $2 billion in comparison.

Coca-Cola claims its recipe is a super-secret and that it is stored in a high-security vault impenetrable to most. That seems like a marketing tactic. There are enough people who claim the recipe is kind of an open secret. And that may be true. Because there are quite a few competitors to Coca-Cola who sell a similar brown-black cola drink in different parts of the world. But none of them have been able to catch on.

The way Coca-Cola works is that it supplies bottled drinks to different parts of the world or supplies the syrup that is later used to make Coca-Cola in different parts of the world. The recipe isn't exactly a secret, it doesn't taste all that different from sugar water and there are clearly no health benefits. Why haven't other beverage makers been able to replace Coca-Cola? Coca-Cola is doing something the others aren't able to. And that something is a mundane-sounding pair of words: distribution network. Then, why don't the others also build it? They're trying very hard.

Over the decades, Coca-Cola invested heavily in developing its network throughout the world. The network that has come to be is so vast, it is practically impossible to replicate it in just a few years. You might be able to guess where this is going. Your investments will be much bigger if you give them time. And if you don't, it'll be very hard for them to become as big.

It's very difficult to build a large corpus of money if you start late. After a point, it is practically impossible. Let's assume you start investing ₹20,000 per month and the return you get is 12 per cent. How much will you have when you're sixty years old? If you start at age thirty-five, you'll have ₹3.8 crores. If you start at age thirty, you'll have ₹7.1 crores. If you start at age twenty-five, you'll have ₹13 crores. Read that again. Look at the difference more time makes.

If you want to start at age thirty-five and, with the same return, end up with ₹13 crores, you'll have to invest ₹70,000 every month. This isn't to say that that's the return you'll get. It's to highlight the importance of work done over time. And not just investments and cola drink distribution networks. The worthwhile things take time to develop: reputation, skills, relations, health ... play the long game.

There's another obvious takeaway for investors from this Coca-Cola edition. Moat. Coca-Cola has something that the others don't. And this ensures that Coca-Cola can survive and thrive much better than its rivals.

9

It's Small Folk Versus the Big Fish

THIS WEEK HAS BEEN eventful. We'll try to keep this very simple. Remember, if you go in deeper, there's a lot more happening than just this. We are referring to short selling. It allows you to make money when the share price is falling. Sounds impossible to those who don't know about it, but it exists. You borrow shares from the broker. Yes, borrow, not buy. There's a small interest that needs to be paid for this borrowing.

Now, you are required to return these shares to the broker at a pre-decided point in the future (remember, you borrowed the stocks; you didn't buy them). So, what you do is:

1. Borrow stocks.
2. Sell them at the current price and get the money.
3. Then, you buy the same number of stocks when their share price falls. So now, you have the same number of stocks you had borrowed. But you paid a lower price. The difference is your profit.
4. You return the stocks to the broker.

You made money from stocks whose price was falling. What could go wrong? A lot can go wrong. What if the price of the stock starts going up? Then you will have to buy the stocks at a higher price – because no matter what, you have to return the stocks you borrowed. There's an even bigger problem. While a stock's price can go down to 0 and stop there, there's no limit to how much it can go up. This means if you were trying to short a stock and it started going up instead of down, theoretically, there's no limit to your losses.

Hedge funds are similar to mutual funds. But there are some noteworthy differences. They both pool money from investors and manage the money. But hedge funds mostly have rich investors. They both invest. But while mutual funds have very narrow and defined investment avenues, hedge funds are much more open and have a lot more freedom. Among the many things they do, hedge funds also short stocks.

Mostly, the short stocks are of companies that are performing poorly and those whose stock prices are expected to fall. A short squeeze is a situation when the price of the stock goes up, leading to losses for those who were shorting the stock. Sometimes, a short squeeze happens on its own, due to some organic reason: a rumour, a temporary rise in hopes or some noteworthy news. Very rarely, it is intentional.

In 1919, there was a company called Piggly Wiggly – a self-service retail store. Some big investors started shorting the stock because they didn't see much value in it. The founder of the company, Clarence Saunders, decided to fight. He borrowed $10 million and started buying his company's shares. This drove the price up, and the shorters faced giant losses. Unfortunately, things didn't end well for him as trading of the stock was suspended and the founder went bankrupt.

Though not intentional, something similar happened with Tesla stock too. But nothing comes close to what happened over the last week in the US markets. Among many, young people in the US tend to have a somewhat negative impression of hedge funds. In a Reddit thread, a bunch of investors decided to start buying the stocks of

GameStop and AMC. Some big hedge funds had placed shorts on them. Some of these hedge funds lost up to 30 per cent of their total. The small-time investors were mostly young people buying stocks. This short squeeze has been publicly praised by many within the financial industry.

There were calls for a similar movement in India on some online groups. But in India, investors aren't as worried about such a thing happening. Our rules are very airtight; brokers and funds in India are highly regulated and their powers are strongly checked. There are restrictions on the positions you can hold and the leverage you can take. US stocks are held by brokers, Indian stocks are kept in demat accounts – away from brokers. Indian brokers can't sell or share order lists.

10

Every Single Star

MERCEDES VERSUS ... WHAT CAME to your mind? BMW? Mercedes versus BMW. The rivalry between Mercedes and BMW is easily one of the top ten rivalries in the corporate world. Both have a car to compete with each other in the hottest segments.

Mercedes makes a vehicle called Unimog. It isn't sold in India. But it is sold in many parts of Europe. It started about seventy years ago as a farm vehicle – a tractor. It's a small truck. It is a vehicle so versatile; it is hard to imagine what it hasn't been used for. It's called the 'Swiss Army knife' of the automobile world.

FIGURE 10.1 Mercedes-Benz Unimog truck

The Unimog has incredible off-road capabilities. It can wade through deep water, climb mountain slopes, operate in the hot Sahara Desert or the north of the Arctic Circle, all while lifting a heavy load. It has been used as a tractor, fire engine, ambulance, home on wheels, army truck, tree trimmer, snow removal vehicle and train engine too! Mercedes also makes trucks, buses and vans. But to most of us, they make luxury lifestyle vehicles.

BMW is also a luxury lifestyle vehicle maker. They make motorcycles and cars. In 2019, Mercedes sold around 2.5 million cars worldwide. BMW did about the same. For whatever reason, Mercedes hasn't ventured into motorcycles. And BMW hasn't tried trucks and buses.

FIGURE 10.2 BMW bike

Nescafé hasn't tried to brew beer. Kingfisher doesn't sell coffee. Tata doesn't make tractors. Maruti doesn't make buses. McDonald's big push isn't pizza. Domino's doesn't really try its hand at burgers. All these competing companies are after the same set of people.

How hard would it be for Domino's to make burgers or for McDonald's to try pizzas? Not exactly easy. But if they wanted to, they probably could. But they don't. Maybe starting that new something would take up too much time and effort.

While many do experiment, and that's good too, it must be noted here that to win big, you have to focus on something. And often, focus means saying no to other things. Quite often, some of the other things you said no to might still do well. You don't have to own every stock that hits the top gainers list every week. As long as you have one very good or a few very good investments, and you know and understand them, you can spare yourself the need to try and invest in every good stock, mutual fund and real estate deal.

11

Investments With and Without Upper Limit

For nearly all athletes, there's a piece of gear that is extremely crucial. If you're a batsman, your bat is crucial. If you're a tennis player, your racket is critical. But nearly all athletes who play a sport standing up agree on one piece of gear being extremely crucial: shoes. (Just in case you're wondering which sports aren't played standing up: they include swimming, cycling and a few more.)

Great shoes haven't been around for more than a century. One of the biggest problems with shoes is that the bottom foam gets compressed over time. It affects the performance of athletes. This was a problem, but it wasn't a big problem. Top athletes could just buy new shoes every single day.

Frank Rudy was an aerospace engineer in the US. He was drafted into the army in 1945 and later worked in the aerospace industry. Frank was an avid inventor. He had over 250 patents to his name. The engineer had an idea that would solve the shoe problem. He approached a couple of companies with this idea. His idea would prevent the soles of shoes from deforming. They all turned him down. He kept pursuing different companies until one of them agreed.

Frank's idea was to get rid of the foam. Balloons don't deform when stressed. Footballs don't deform. Car tyres don't deform. Air doesn't deform. Instead of foam that deforms over time, he wanted to use a small bag of air in the shoes, and Nike Air was born. Nike makes many shoes. The Nike Air line has a huge following that many other shoe lines of Nike don't enjoy.

This was the mid-1970s. A couple of years later, a designer had the grand idea to make the airbag visible from the side of the shoe. Pretty fast, Nike Air became a shoe widely accepted and greatly praised. Nike's bet on air-cushioning technology had paid off. This was something Nike's rivals had failed to capitalise on even though Frank had approached many of them before reaching Nike.

What did Nike see in Frank's technology that the other companies didn't? Well, we don't know what Nike saw. What Nike does is something nearly all great investors do as well. Have you heard of Nike Shox? These are shoes that have a spring-like mechanism in them. They didn't catch on much; not all investments catch on.

If you go down Nike's history, you will come across many shoes. Very few of them became super successful. Some were absolute failures. Many were somewhere in between. And it's anyone's guess, they all would have cost a similar amount to develop.

If a shoe line fails, Nike loses the money it spent on development. And then moves on. If the shoe line does average, it recoups its initial cost and moves on. If the shoe line succeeds, they print money by the bucket-load. Experimentation costs them a small amount. Success brings money. The highest possible loss they can suffer is whatever amount they invested. The highest gain they could make is multiple times their investment. That's how you should plan your investment.

No matter how good things are, certain investments will only give you so much in return. But some will climb up as though there were no upper limit. Of all your investments, which are likely to go to zero and stop? All of them? But which are likely to go up to a certain limit and stop? Some of them are. But not all. Make sure you invest in such investments too.

12

Stick to What Suits You

IN 1964, A NEW train was introduced in Japan called the Shinkansen. You might have heard its more popular name – the bullet train. At launch, it could touch a speed of 210 kmph. Japan had spent preposterous amounts of money developing the train and building tracks for it. These high-speed trains require long stretches of straight lines.

The Japanese built straight lines cutting through hills, tunnelling and building bridges. It was a massive success. Seeing this, the French started work on something similar. They developed the TGV. It came out in 1981, and it could go up to 260 kmph.

The French too did it the Japanese way. They laid new tracks which were long and straight. In the UK, they couldn't build new straight tracks. The country already had a vast railway network. At the same time, due to the increasing popularity of cars and planes, fewer people were riding trains. The UK's rail network was also very old. Designed for much slower steam trains from a century ago, it had many bends – something that prevented trains from going fast. In 1969, the British Rail started work on the Advanced Passenger Train (APT). They couldn't change the tracks, so they did something nobody had ever done before.

When you ride a motorcycle or scooter around a bend, what do you do to maintain speed when going around a corner? You lean or tilt. Bikes lean into a bend. Cars don't. The APT was designed to actively tilt into bends like a two-wheeler.

Once you're done reading this, go and search for a video of the tilting train. They look quite elegant leaning into bends — quite unreal if you've never seen it before. It used computers to sense the bends and tilt accordingly.

With this technology, the APT could go into corners at nearly twice the normal speed. Its top speed was 260 kmph. In 1981, the APT train was put to the test in the UK. Almost instantly, several things started to fail. The ride was jarring, the train was constantly rattling, the brakes had issues a few times, there were breakdowns and it made riders feel queasy.

They took it away for three years. After that, they reintroduced the train. By then, the train had received enough bad press. And things just didn't seem to work. They stopped it. In 1982, British Rail sold the patents of the APT train to the company Fiat. And that was the end of it. The UK didn't get a high-speed train.

In the late 1990s, a certain entrepreneur, Richard Branson, wanted to solve the prevalent problem in the UK. Richard is famous for the brand Virgin — Virgin Airlines and Virgin Mobile. He ran Virgin Trains in the UK. While doing research in Italy, he found a particular train model called Pendolino.

Italy, like the UK, had tracks that weren't very straight. And yet, the Pendolino was able to move at super high speeds across them. He signed a deal for the Pendolino train. In 2001, Virgin Trains introduced the UK to high-speed railway: the Pendolino train had reached the UK. The new train would ply on the same routes that the APT was supposed to. So, how did the Pendolino solve the problem that the tilting APT couldn't solve? This is very peculiar. Pendolino was a train made by Fiat. They used the technology bought from British Rail back in 1982. The Pendolino was a tilting train. Just like the APT.

That technology didn't work for British Rail, but it worked for the Pendolino train. Today, Pendolino trains are used in Italy, Spain, Germany, Switzerland, Russia, China, just to name a few countries. And yes, even in the UK. There are countries where the Pendolino train works wonders. But in the rest of the world, they still don't make much sense. There are investment methods that work for many. And then there are investment methods that work for a few. If something works for you, it doesn't matter if it doesn't work for others.

A very popular method of investing in stocks is to buy stocks of high-quality companies. Analyse their business, analyse their cashflow, see what the company is doing and what it plans to do, see how good the management team is, check everything about the company, buy the stock and hold it for a very long period. This seems to work for a lot of investors. There are many other techniques. One of them is called momentum investing. It is more nuanced than this but to put it simply: invest looking at the trend.

Trends tend to hold for some time so stick with the trend. Is the stock going up? Keep investing in it. Is it going down? Short it. There's no need to look at the underlying company's business. This isn't exactly a new form of investing, and many investors swear by it. In fact, there are enough tests to show that it manages to give better returns over a period of 200 years. But there's a catch: momentum investors tend to see very high returns at certain times. And in other times, the returns are abysmal. In March 2020, when the markets had massively plunged, scores of investors couldn't handle it. Many sold. Many waited for a few days and then sold.

This is why, for many, the momentum strategy doesn't make money – they aren't able to deal with the ups and downs. For many investors, such swings are not worth it. However, there are some who make a lot of money using it. With this imparting, the intention is not to encourage you to try the momentum strategy. The intention is to make you explore and see what works for you. There's nothing wrong with any investment style. The one that suits you is the one you can live with.

13

When Does a Bubble Pop?

You or your family own a house. That or your landlord owns the house. Either way, the price of the house is of great importance to you (rents are somewhat in tandem with house prices). Unless you're very rich, you will need to take a loan when you're buying a house.

In Australia, in the 1950s, if an average person wanted to buy a house in a big city (Melbourne, Sydney), it would take them around three years to pay back the loan.[1] In the 1980s, the Australian government made a few minor changes to the laws governing interest rates. Around the same time, housing prices started to rise. Money poured in. New houses were made. Their prices climbed up too.

Towards the end of the 1980s, it would take an average person around five years to pay back the loan for a house as opposed to the 1950s. This was higher than what Australians were used to. This is where many started to believe that the prices were unsustainably high. Many expected a crash. Years passed and the prices kept climbing.

In 1999, something happened that shook the markets. Back then, people would buy any stock with .com at the end of it. The internet was brand new. Everybody wanted a piece of this revolution. Investors (mainly in the US) bought and raised the prices of technology stocks to astronomical values. The dot-com bubble hit.

Every random technology stock with a high valuation fell. Good companies too went down with them. Surely, with the markets affected, overpriced assets would see their bubbles burst. In 2000, it would take an average person around five years to pay back the loan for a city house in Australia. Nothing had changed and the prices had not fallen.

In fact, by 2003, this number had climbed to seven years. Then, in 2008, the housing loan crisis hit the US markets and shocked the world. It would now take an average person around seven years to pay back the loan for a city house in Australia. They hadn't crashed. The bubble was very much intact. In 2010, this number touched eight years.

The period between 2010 and 2020 was filled with dire predictions. Every single year, people expected a major crash. But the bubble remained. In 2020, the pandemic hit. The entire world shut down. Nothing like it had ever been witnessed before.

After nearly forty years, the bubble was destined to burst – or so they believed. It did not. You can search on the internet to see what predictions were made for 2021. The point is, it still costs an average person in Australia more than seven years of income to buy a house. Sure, the prices haven't been steady. There have been some corrections. But the average person there still can't buy a house with three years of income. It still takes around seven years' worth of income.

Why isn't the bubble bursting? There are many arguments. Many of these arguments suggest that the higher prices are being artificially kept up. Some argue that there are laws that prevent higher buildings from coming up, laws that prevent newer land from being acquired, laws that make taxation easier, very cheap loans and such reasons. All of that doesn't matter. Artificially or not, the fact is, the prices have remained high for forty years.

Several people there have spent years waiting for the burst to buy a house. Many stopped waiting and bought a house. As an investor, you must realise, the markets often don't make sense. And while you'd expect them to eventually make sense, there are no guaranteed time frames. Something can continue to not make sense for longer than you can remain sane. As an investor, you must choose an investment strategy that doesn't depend on a crash or burst to make the right move.

Some investment strategies work through ups and downs. Some work only in specific periods. Know what you're getting into. You already must know how almost nobody has a good track record in predicting crashes. There is a very famous quote by John Maynard Keynes: 'The markets can remain irrational longer than you can remain solvent.'[2] And then there is the other side of this argument. What if the Australian city prices are high but they're high because there is real demand? What if the sunny weather, friendly neighbours and yellow sand beaches have resulted in more people moving there year after year to settle? What if, just what if, what you think is a bubble, isn't a bubble at all?

14

The Thin Line Between Crazy Good and Just Crazy

You're going to a new place. You've never been there before. What kind of place would you choose to live in? A good hotel? Online reviews showing hundreds of positive comments? A famous hotel brand name? Sounds good.

Would you stay in a stranger's house? You probably said no. About ten years ago, most people would have said no. But Airbnb thought you would stay in a stranger's house. They went on to make it their business model. The idea was so crazy, nobody else was doing it. Since nobody was doing it, Airbnb had almost no competition.

Today, they are practically the only company in the space. They have more rooms than any hotel chain, and they have a market cap bigger than any hotel company in the world. Airbnb took a contrarian bet.

Contrarian ideas are those that nobody or very few are in favour of. If too many people agree on an idea, it can't be contrarian. During a Vanity Fair New Establishment Summit, Jeff Bezos claimed, 'Here's the thing about contrarians. They're mostly wrong.'[1] He then goes on to acknowledge that some of Amazon's best outcomes were contrarian moves.

In investing too, contrarian bets have the potential to pay off big and handsome prizes. But that doesn't come from merely being against whatever everyone else is doing.

It comes from truly understanding something that nobody else has understood yet. Contrarian ideas are ideas that only a few people have thought of. Hence, they appear bizarre. And therefore, they're indistinguishable from ideas that really are crazy and have no future.

There is no lack of absolutely crazy ideas. There's a company that freezes people's bodies after their death and stores them.[2] The hope is that someday, when the medical technology is advanced enough, they will unfreeze the bodies and perform medical procedures to cure the dead person and bring them back to life. Would this work? We don't know. But this is an absolutely wild idea very few people seem to be doing. If it works, life and death will never be viewed the same again.

15

Formula to Hold the Best Performers

MOST OF US WOULD love to see a multibagger stock in our portfolio. And why not? There's one multibagger that has outperformed beyond the wildest imaginations of investors: 38 per cent per annum for twenty-three years. An investment of ₹1 lakh at the start would have grown to ₹15.76 crore today. Yes, we're talking about Amazon.

The sad part of that stock's story is that almost no investor has enjoyed the stellar return (except Jeff Bezos and a small number of others who work there and aren't really investors). Why? Simply because the journey of the stock was as wild as its returns. There were many other years when the stock took a massive beating. To top this, the company wasn't making any profits for decades.

There is an early interview of Jeff Bezos where a journalist appears very sceptical of his company's operations.[1] Many analysts called it 'not a viable company' for years altogether. There were times when its stock was down 95 per cent. If you had invested around 2000, your stocks would be in the red for eight years. Would you have held for that long? Think again, would you have held on to it when it fell 95 per cent? Probably not.

So now the question is how exactly do you hold on to such a stock? What signs should you look for in the company's balance sheets? What are the most important ratios? What do you look for?

A little more than a century ago, if you broke your bone, the cure for it would be surprisingly similar to what it is today. Bones tend to break in a manner that is surprisingly similar in people of similar age. The bones would be realigned, plaster would be applied and, quite a few weeks later, your broken bone would have fused into one piece again.

Hairline fractures were difficult to trace. The pain would remain for long and nobody would be able to find the source of the pain. With time, the crack or hairline fracture would heal. As you can imagine, the cracks would never heal properly because not much was done to realign and make the bone fully straight. Even with big fractures, the healed bones wouldn't always turn out to be as good as before.

Wilhelm Roentgen, a physicist in Bavaria, was experimenting with cathode ray tubes.[2] He wanted to see if a certain kind of light would pass through glass. The light managed to clear the glass and hit a fluorescent screen. Mind you, the screen just happened to be there. It wasn't really a part of his experiment. Observing what happened on the screen, he realised that the mysterious light that he wasn't even able to see could pass through glass and many other objects. But it failed to pass through hard objects. And that is how X-rays were discovered.

Within a year, hospitals across the globe were using it to treat bone injuries, kidney stones and bullet wounds. He got a Nobel Prize in Physics in 1901 for his discovery. So how did he do it? He didn't really have a plan. It just happened. When you're looking for a stock that shoots from nothing to insane prices, there is no rule book. There are no signs or numbers that you can look at that guarantee success. It's very difficult to bet on success unless it is in hindsight. And this is why looking for the next Amazon cannot be your only investment strategy, because it is mostly not going to work out.

For most investors, investing in stocks that make sense and staying away from stocks that don't make sense is the best strategy. There are many investors who have made good money by investing in Amazon stock around ten years ago – when it started to make sense to them, and the Amazon stock has served them pretty well: 34 per cent per annum in the last ten years.

Don't be harsh on yourself for not having seen what practically nobody could see. Warren Buffett is a big fan of Jeff Bezos and yet he never invested in Amazon stock.

16

The Missing Link That Negates All Else

WHEN TWO SIDES FIGHT and nothing is stopping them, a clear victor emerges pretty soon. In real life though, there are always things stopping the two sides. During the unfortunate period last century when the Second World War took place, there were two main sides: the Allies and the Axis.

The Allied powers consisted mainly of the US, the UK, Russia and several other countries. The Axis powers consisted mainly of Germany, Italy and Japan. Towards the end of the Second World War, the Axis powers were retreating while the Allied powers charged ahead against them. The Axis couldn't exactly fight the Allied forces. With backing from the US, the Allies had access to armaments that the Axis couldn't compete with.

The Allies had the Air Force that could go deep into Axis territory and drop bombs. Air-dropped bombs can cause great damage. But they are somehow never enough to truly defeat the other side. For a war to truly have a winner and loser, the land needs to be controlled by one side. In defence circles, there's a common agreement: you can only control land with tanks.

The Axis side had a formidable tank called the Tiger tank. The Allies developed an answer to this called the Churchill tank. This is where the Axis powers pulled off a neat trick because they couldn't fight the Churchill tank. But what if the Churchill tank never reached them?

The terrain in Europe has many small rivers and streams, and they destroyed nearly all of the bridges over them.

The Churchill tank weighed 36 tonnes. How does a tank cross a river? It needs a bridge; without a bridge, it didn't matter if the Churchill tank existed or not. You can also have soldiers cross the rivers and streams on boats with light vehicles like Jeeps. Unfortunately, those soldiers on Jeeps, upon crossing the river, would come face-to-face with a tank. A tank called the Tiger tank, no less.

Building a bridge was the only way forward. How long does that take? A conventional bridge is something no army has time for. So they developed an unconventional bridge: a Bailey Bridge. A Bailey Bridge is very similar to a Lego toy. Its main piece is a rectangular structure with two squares inside it at 45 degrees. These pieces can be attached to each other using pins. Each of these weighed only around 250 kilograms which meant around six people could lift it, no cranes needed. It also meant that it could be carried in small trucks to very remote locations.

FIGURE 16.1 Bailey Bridge built during the Second World War

The Missing Link That Negates All Else

A Bailey Bridge can be built by a bunch of soldiers without any cranes in a matter of hours. Today, many armies across the world use it. The Indian Army uses it too. Without going too deep into unfortunate wartime stories, the Bailey Bridge enabled the Allies to use their tanks. The Allied had everything done correctly except one thing: the bridge. That missing link, when solved, allowed them to use whatever else they had done correctly.

You can do everything right, and none of that will matter if key parts are missing. Like many lessons from life, this fits perfectly in the investing world too. You might have chosen the best funds to invest in, and then not have an emergency fund.

You could have picked absolute winner stocks, and not gotten yourself medical insurance. There could be a weak link that effectively negates all the things you have done right. Find it and build a Bailey Bridge over it!

17

How Many Winners Can There Be?

In the 1990s, a young boy in Ireland was infamous for getting into fights at school. After every fight, he would think deeply about the fight — about the punches he'd hit and the punches he'd been hurt by. One day, a group of seniors decided to beat him black and blue. The ambush scarred the young boy. Shaken by the experience, he decided to take up mixed martial arts to defend himself.

His mind was never really in school or academics. When he grew up, he became a plumber. But he never gave up martial arts. Disagreeing strongly with his parents, the boy gave up plumbing and pursued mixed martial arts full-time. In 2007, he got the break he needed. He debuted in the Irish Ring of Truth.

He was fighting against another amateur fighter. He knocked out his competitor in just the first round. A year later, he was signed professionally and fought his first fight as a professional fighter. He won it. He went on to win all of the next eight fights he fought. And not just win, he finished each of those fights within two rounds. His opponents in those fights couldn't last beyond the second round. He had been preparing for these days since he was a little boy. Fighting was all he ever thought of. And now, that unwavering dedication was paying off.

In 2013, the Ultimate Fighting Championship (UFC) signed him up. For those who follow UFC, the first line of this chapter would have been enough to conclude that this person is Conor McGregor.

In his first UFC fight, Conor won against his opponent in less than a minute. He was known to finish fights before their time was up because his opponents were either too injured or gave up much earlier than all the rounds were over. When he fought for the belt in the featherweight category, he finished the match by knocking out his opponent. But that's normal for Conor. What's not normal for any fight is this: the fight started, and thirteen seconds later, it was over. At this point, Conor McGregor could boast of an achievement very few fighters could boast of – he hadn't lost a single fight in the last ten years.

In March 2016, he decided to fight someone from two weight classes above him. He was up against a much heavier Nate Diaz. At this point, Conor had fifteen wins to his name. Fifteen wins, and no losses. However, he lost to Nate – Conor's first loss in the UFC. In August of the same year, he was back in the ring. He wasn't just back fighting; he was back to fight Nate Diaz. And this time, Conor defeated Nate Diaz.

After this, Conor McGregor took some time off to prepare for the birth of his first child. His inactivity meant he lost the featherweight and lightweight class belts he had earned. Away from UFC, Conor decided to give boxing a shot. He challenged Floyd Mayweather – the number one boxer at that time – but Conor lost in that fight.

With a fight that big, Conor still earned $100 million. While this was happening, there was a new rising star in the UFC – Khabib Nurmagomedov. Khabib was a Russian fighter who was climbing the ranks fast. He earned the belt in the lightweight category – a belt once held by Conor. Khabib also had never lost a match.

In October 2018, the two formidable fighters, Conor and Khabib, met eye to eye in the ring. 'I want to change his face,' Khabib is famous for saying before the match.[1] It was a brutal match, but by the fourth round, Khabib had defeated Conor. Conor lost the belt and Khabib remained undefeated.

The world of wrestling, fighting and boxing is such. There are winners, and there are losers. Unknown to most of us, for every famous fighter we see spar on our screens, there are thousands who try but never come close to becoming famous. Conor McGregor admitted to living on social support until his first fight got him some bonus money – that's how little money he had.

There are some investments that are a zero-sum game – quite like fighting. There are winners and there are losers. Then there are others where there can be multiple winners and fewer losers. Trading is a zero-sum game. Some make money, others lose money. Long-term investing is not a zero-sum game. If everybody stays patiently invested, they all can make money. There's no right or wrong. Conor is extremely good at what he does. For him, it makes perfect sense to fight in a zero-sum game environment. For many others, it is not. And this applies to not just investing. When you play a game, make sure you know how many winners there can be.

18

Some Winners Keep Winning

Jerry Nyman is a programmer working for a school's transportation department. His job is to mainly ensure the schoolkids' paths are safe while boarding school buses and walking to bus stops. Besides physically surveying locations, he also uses Google Maps to look at routes and paths. One day, while looking at an area with many bungalows and a lake, he noticed something peculiar.

In one of the water bodies behind a row of villas, he observed a certain shape under the water. It seemed like it was a car. He knew someone in the area and gave that person a call. He asked her to check what it was. That lady involved her neighbour who went to check and indeed, it was a car submerged underwater.

With the help of the police, they pulled out the car. In the car, they found a skeleton in the driver's seat. With some difficulty, they were able to ascertain the identity of the skeleton. It was a man named William Moldt.[1] His relatives finally got the closure they had so eagerly wanted. They had, for years, wondered what had happened to William. And for years, the police hadn't been able to solve the case. In September 2019, a programmer helped bring an end to this mystery. William had gone partying, got drunk and drove himself into the lake without anyone ever finding him. This had taken place in 1997.

This is a glamorous example of just how good Google Maps are. There are many far less glamorous but more widespread uses of Google Maps. Ola or Uber wouldn't work without Google Maps. They pay a hefty fee to Google to use their maps. The same goes for Swiggy, Zomato and numerous other businesses. How many people have you heard of who use Apple Maps, Bing Maps or TomTom? That's because Google Maps is far better than its closest rivals. It isn't just better; it keeps getting better with time.

Millions use Google Maps every day to navigate the world, and Google Maps uses its user's data to improve its maps. This is a good formula: the more users use Google Maps, the better it gets. The better it gets; the more users use it. In 2008, Google started a project called Street View where they sent cars with roof-mounted cameras around the streets of the world. With these high-resolution pictures, Google had a bank of data like nobody else. It then used satellite imagery of the world to mark roads and buildings.

Combining the data from its Street View with the satellite imagery, Google achieved the first version of Google Maps. Nobody had made anything as good before. Many of their competitors could buy satellite imagery. Nobody could buy the data Google had accumulated over the years via its Street View project. Apple stepped into the arena and launched Apple Maps. Gradually, Apple improved its software and big data capabilities. It was soon able to mark out buildings, bungalows and other such large structures.

By the time Apple had done so, Google had already moved much ahead – Google Maps was able to mark out even tiny sheds. Other maps are getting better. But nobody is getting better than Google Maps. And because no other service is getting better, nobody truly uses anything other than Google Maps.

Little is known about a man named Justin O'Beirne, but it is almost certain he used to work at Apple. In 2018, he talked about Google Maps. He went deep into why Google Maps was so difficult to beat and why, despite its best attempts, Apple had failed to do so. He called it Google Maps' moat. When you're picking stocks, you want to look for companies that, besides having a good balance sheet, management, market share, etc., also have this thing called … moat.

19

What Changed While You Were Looking at the Stock Price

EVERY YEAR, FLOODS RAVAGE great portions of the world causing great losses, suffering and inconvenience; for example, the 2021 floods affecting Bihar and Assam. Nearly every single year, people abandon their villages to temporarily live on higher ground. They often aren't able to carry all their belongings from the houses they leave behind. Some pets die, some get lost. Mind you, in some cases, pets aren't just pets, they're also a source of income — cows, goats and chickens. And then there's the lifestyle that comes with living in such a region.

If you knew your area would be submerged underwater for a few days or weeks, would you buy many big, expensive items? Like a fridge, TV or car? Would you set up a factory to manufacture small items? The floods affect every decision a person residing here has to make, that is the nature of the land. Until the floods in this region are stopped, the people will have to live accordingly. Their minds are programmed to expect floods every year. And this flooding has been taking place for centuries — nothing much ever changes.

The Dutch people live in the Netherlands. The Dutch tend to use cycles to get around more than most other countries because a good portion of the country is easy to cycle on — the country is incredibly flat. Where it is situated, the Netherlands faces a problem that many

What Changed While You Were Looking at the Stock Price 57

other countries face, but the Netherlands faces it more than others – flooding and land erosion. The seas have been biting away chunks of land for long. The Dutch, though, are not running away. The seas are mighty, fierce and harsh, and the Dutch are fighting it by building dikes which are walls of land with water on both sides.

Dikes first came into existence about 500 years ago. These walls prevent water from flowing across and therefore prevent erosion. Over the years, the Dutch set up water pumps powered by windmills and drained the water trapped away from the sea. On this drained piece of land, they started farming. They created new land out of the sea, but this was still a relatively small operation until 1932.

In 1932, they built a massive dike across a big portion of the sea. And since then, they've been reclaiming bits and pieces of land inside this dike-enclosed lake. Almost 17 per cent of the Netherlands is land that used to be sea,[1] which is around 7,000 square kilometres. How big is that? It is nearly twice the size of the entire state of Goa.

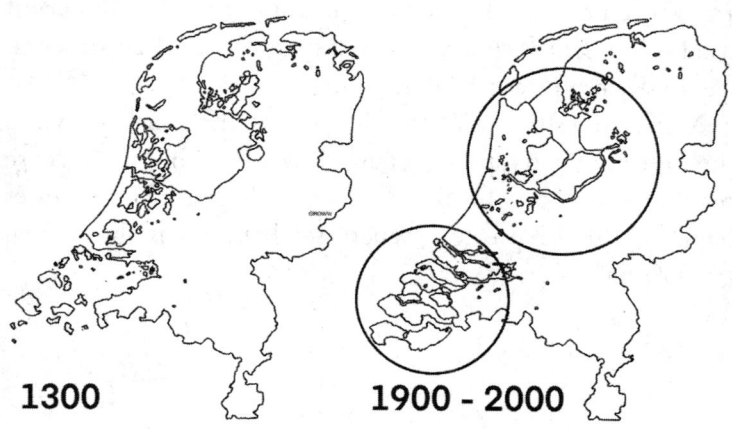

Map not to scale

FIGURE 19.1 The Dutch created new land out of the sea

There was a point in time when the country was worried about how it would feed its growing population. Today, it has so much that it is the second-largest exporter of food in the world. The first is the US (a country which is over 200 times larger).² Where do things stand today? The world's seas are rising and land is being lost. But the Dutch are fighting and winning. They have plans chalked out till beyond the year 2100.

In investing, when the price of certain stocks or the markets generally climb, there's a tendency to expect the markets to fall back to an older level. When the markets reach a certain high, some people stop buying because they expect the markets to fall. This is quite like the floods we see in most places of the world. The floods go away, but they'll come back soon. Many of our minds are programmed like this. Unless the land is changed, like in the Netherlands. Then the floods aren't coming back.

When the markets or certain stocks go up or down, the question we all need to ask is: what has changed? Has the underlying economy or company changed? Have things changed on the ground? If things are more or less the same, then the stock price will possibly return to where it used to be. But if they have changed, the markets or stock has reached a new fair level.

Many investors tend to stay out of the markets when the best climbs happen because they think the markets are overvalued or overheated. Fair enough, that can and does happen. But very often, what also happens is that actual growth has taken place.

20

How One of the Greatest Authors in History Invested His Money

MARK TWAIN IS CONSIDERED to be the father of American literature. He is also known as the greatest humourist America ever produced. Many of his books remain popular even today. For someone who was alive mainly in the 1800s, the admiration he's earned over three different centuries is commendable.

Today we read newspapers, magazines and books without ever thinking much about what goes into them. In the 1800s, printing text quickly on paper was a challenge that inventors were aching to solve. In 1874, James Paige developed and received a patent for the Paige Compositor – a machine to solve this problem. It required only one operator to handle it which was unheard of at that time. The machine was immensely complicated – it had 18,000 different parts.

Mesmerised by the beauty and mechanical complexity, Mark Twain decided to invest in the Paige Compositor in 1880. He called James Paige the 'Shakespeare of mechanical invention'.[1] The problem with this machine was that it required continuous adjustment for errors, so it wasn't deemed ready.

Over an extraordinarily long period of a decade, Paige continued to work on the machine. Twain continued to grow more impatient. Twain, the brilliant writer that he was, knew nothing about mechanics and very little about business.

According to their contract, Mark Twain was entitled to the profits from the machine only if he funded Paige till the end of the development of the machine. The contract did not say anything about how long Paige could take to finish the work. Additionally, Twain had agreed to pay Paige a regular sum of money until the machine turned a profit. Twain grew to hate Paige. But whenever he met Paige, he'd be easily convinced. 'He could persuade a fish to come out and take a walk with him,' said Mark.

Eventually, only two machines were built. And by the time they were ready, their technology was outdated. Mark took over Paige's company along with a businessman friend and tried to turn it around. The friend tried and realised it was a dead end. He cut his losses and asked Mark to shut it down. Twain was willing to blow more money. He said, 'He felt connected to the machine as though it were a person.'

Mark Twain lost all his investment in the Paige Compositor. This wasn't his first bad investment (nor his last). His writings were so good, he accumulated wealth rapidly. His investments were so poor, he lost his accumulated wealth rapidly too. The bad investments spanned across assets — gold mines to startups to venture investments to stocks to bonds. The shame of having made a bad decision made him latch on to his investments and delay the losses in the hope of recovery. In most of his investments, there never was a recovery, only a deepening of losses.

In investing, emotions have very little room. You cannot continue making a bad investment because of shame or excitement or nostalgia or overconfidence or the multitude of other emotions that rule our minds. You cannot choose an investment because you simply 'feel' it will do well. But humans are emotional creatures so we must deliberately sit and review our decisions. And while reviewing, we should remove as many emotions from our decisions as we can.

Toward the end of the 1800s, Mark Twain had to take loans to support himself and his lifestyle. He was a man who was sensitive to what the public thought of him and at that point in his life, newspapers had written so much about his poor choices and debt that he was shaken. He promised to pay back every single penny.

Twain set off on a grand tour doing what he was good at. He was good at humour, and he performed the world over in what might now be described as stand-up comedy shows. The American writer travelled all over the world – from South Africa to Europe, from Australia to India. He managed to pay back all his dues and make even more money for himself.

After paying back his dues, when he had money lying around, he again invested. This time, it was in a cashier company. In around eight months, he realised it was going nowhere. This time, he decided to swallow his pride and cut his losses.

21

Where Does Your Advisor Invest?

Jungles command a certain mysterious allure. Most human beings live outside jungles and the vastness, the dampness, the unusual sounds, the ever-present threat of danger, all contribute to a jungle's mysteries. In remote jungles and forests, even today, scientists are discovering new species of animals, plants, minerals and remains of older civilisations.

In 1993, a man named Guzman had big news from Busang, a jungle in Indonesia. He had found gold in vast quantities. The same year a mining company, Bre-X, bought land in Busang and started drilling. It was rumoured that this piece of land had the biggest deposit of gold ever found on Earth and tests were conducted to verify the claims.

The tests came back positive; the land did contain good amounts of gold. The fire caught on in Wall Street. JP Morgan, Fidelity, Invesco and some other big names from Wall Street talked about the stock in a positive light and investors lined up to buy the stock for a penny. It went from being around $0.30 per share to around $250 per share.

There was a slight hiccup in between. The gold found in the region had characteristic rounded edges. The project manager, Guzman, explained that the gold was rounded in nature due to the 'volcanic pool' theory (a fake theory he used to convince investors). With that problem sorted, the work continued. In 1996, the Indonesian government revoked the permits for the operation. Their accusation was that the company wasn't playing by the rules of the country.

By now, many mining companies and several big investors from all over the world wanted a share of this gold. To solve the deadlock with the government, a joint venture was formed in which, besides Bre-X, the Indonesian government was also a stakeholder. Now, work could start again.

Oddly, just before work restarted, there was a fire and a good portion of records was lost. At this point, the third company in the venture decided to continue work and redo whatever tests were necessary. The reports came back and there was almost no gold to be found in Busang. The stock went from around $250 back to being a penny stock.

The auditors wanted to talk to the man who knew this area very well; the man who found the gold here in the first place – the project manager, Guzman. He jumped from the helicopter, dying by suicide on his way to meet the auditors.[1] It was later learned that he had started by filing away his wedding ring into samples. Later, he bought gold additionally to mix with the samples.

There was no gold. When investors had asked Bre-X about the region, the company had replied positively. Unfortunately for the investors, there was nobody else they could have asked to verify the claims except Bre-X. Before all this was discovered, Guzman, the chief executive officer (CEO), and a few others had sold their stock options, worth over $100 million each – something they never told anyone.

The company had lied to investors to benefit themselves. While everybody was buying the stock, they were selling it. When someone tells you where to invest, it might be worth asking them to show where they invest. The famous thinker and author, Nassim Taleb, talks about this in his book *Skin in the Game*. He believes people who don't have skin in the game shouldn't be advising others to get in the game.

Many advisors (in the investment world or otherwise) make recommendations to others while not having exposure to the risks involved. Such people are not vulnerable to the effects of the game going wrong. Nassim Taleb is famous for these lines in his book: 'Don't tell me what you think, show me your portfolio.'

22

The Man Who Gives the Most

IN 1945, A MAN named Mohamed started a business manufacturing cooking oil and soap in Amalner, Maharashtra. The same year, his son was born. Two years later, India got its independence. The business did well and the family prospered. Mohamed decided to send his son to study abroad at one of the best universities in the world – Stanford University.

Mohamed unexpectedly passed away in 1996. His son was only twenty-one years old and had to take over the business. Despite being so young and inexperienced, he was able to lead the company to newer heights. From making just vegetable oil and soap, the company expanded to making lighting products, baby products, toiletries and hydraulic cylinders.

In the 1980s, the company entered information technology sector. At this point, the company's name didn't seem very apt – Western Indian Vegetable Products Ltd. The name was shortened and changed to Wipro. The young twenty-one-year-old who took over the company from his father was Azim Premji. Wipro manufactured minicomputers and gradually, over time, became a software company.

Wipro has now become one of the biggest companies in India. In its latest quarterly results, the company declared a profit of ₹2,972 crore. Today, Azim Premji is a billionaire and one of the richest people in India.

But that's not what makes him different. What makes him different is his habit of giving money away – philanthropy. In 2020 alone, he donated ₹7,904 crore. In fact, Azim Premji has been consistent with his donations for a long time. So far, he's said to have given away around 35 per cent of his net worth.

He is the number one donor in India. The next person, the second in line, donated only one-tenth of that amount in 2020.

The world today is in a poor situation due to the pandemic. India is experiencing a second wave right now. Many other countries experienced their second wave a few months ago. In this second wave, there are many areas where each one of us can help and we should.

The easiest and most convenient way is to donate some amount; it doesn't matter how much. You don't have to match Azim Premji. Yes, he's a giant in his contributions and that has an impact. But that doesn't mean a much smaller amount doesn't have an impact. The second wave in India has brought forward so many tales of generosity displayed by fellow Indians. An auto-rickshaw driver in Bhopal installed an oxygen cylinder and an oximeter in his vehicle. He ferries critical patients to the hospital for free.[1] A beedi maker from Kerala donated ₹2 lakh during the pandemic. Last year when the pandemic started, a daily-wage-working woman spent all her money from that day's earnings to buy juice bottles for the policemen working to ensure social distancing in her area. Her contribution is minuscule compared to Azim Premji's. And yet, her contribution made a real impact.

Even a small donation equivalent to one day's earnings or a few days' worth of earnings has a real impact. It doesn't matter which organisation you donate to – NGO, local government, central government or any other organisation. What matters is that you donate.

23

Chase the Life and Not the Lifestyle

CIGARETTE SMOKING IS INJURIOUS to health. Yes, we know this all too well today but there was a time when the general public wasn't so sure. Around the 1950s, against the wishes of some companies, new research surfaced: cigarettes are bad.[1] Cigarette brands were suddenly panicking. How would they sell? Many big brands resorted to measures they hoped would be enough which included better filters, lesser tobacco content, higher-quality paper. The marketing campaign for them was equally hyped. But none of these actually proved to make cigarette smoking noticeably safer.

A particular cigarette brand decided to approach the problem differently. In their marketing material, they barely even spoke about their cigarette – something nobody had done. How is it an advertisement about a product if you don't even talk about the product? They portrayed a very manly cowboy, going about his tough and rugged lifestyle – feeding milk to a foal, caring for and playing with his horses on a farm.

People loved it. Everybody wanted to be that man. Or at least, they wanted others to think they were that man. The cowboy was running with his horses, feeding a foal, caring for his animals. Many would like to do that, but most wouldn't go so far as buying a farm and then living on it. He was also smoking this brand's cigarette. That's easy. Most people could do that.

FIGURE 23.1 Marlboro cowboy advertisement

The company went from being a name nobody knew to being the top tobacco brand in the world – Marlboro. With the cowboy lifestyle ad, Marlboro had started lifestyle marketing. Lifestyle marketing is more common than you realise.[2] Nike ads don't talk about how good their shoes are; they show an athletic person going through the mental and physical struggles of a sportsperson.

Red Bull doesn't talk much about the drink it makes. It just plasters its logo all over events attended by young folks – Formula 1 racing, mountain biking, aerial acrobatics, concerts. Apple doesn't talk about how much memory the iPhone has. It just produces ads that make you want to be the person in the ad. Similarly, Coca-Cola doesn't tell you about their drink; they just show happy and excited people drinking Coca-Cola. Marlboro didn't invent anything here. It just discovered it.

If you want to know more about this campaign, search 'Marlboro man' on the internet. Have you looked at a policeman as a kid and thought he was really cool?

Have you wanted to wear that uniform and walk around making sure your neighbourhood was safe? That's you wanting a certain lifestyle. Have you felt like dressing similarly to how industrial tycoons dress? You imagine yourself being that person because you imagine their lifestyle is desirable and the most easily attainable part of their lifestyle is what you first get. Can you build the factories and offices the tycoon has? Maybe, but it'll take time. Can you dress like that person? Yes, very easily. So that's where you start.

A great number of our aspirations are driven by our cravings for a certain lifestyle. Whether this is acceptable in life or not is a debate for another day. But the one place it isn't acceptable at all is investing. Many people are made to think investing is about constantly buying and selling stocks, but it is about having multiple screens with graphs on them, it's about constantly tracking every single move the market makes and always taking action – these are easy to do. It has amplified even more with the rising popularity of trading all the time as the cost of acquiring a smartphone or computer with good internet is very low. Actual investing isn't about these activities.

FIGURE 23.2 Investing requires researching and thinking

In actual investing, these activities are a result of what happens before that: learning, researching and thinking. A lot of times, investing is actually about not doing anything at all – just waiting. As a new investor, make sure that you do this right. Don't chase the investor lifestyle. Be an actual investor.

24

Korean Shipbuilding

In the 1970s, the demand for large ships was declining globally. The world didn't need as many ships as currently existed. The biggest shipbuilders were mainly present in Western Europe and Japan and they started to struggle. In the European nations and Japan, there had been a great demand for ships, so the shipbuilding industries in those countries developed over time.

Around the same time, a small nation, with a landmass smaller than that of the Indian state of Tamil Nadu had a new goal – South Korea wanted to build giant ships. The South Koreans had little experience building very large ships, simply because there wasn't any demand for such ships inside the small country. The Government of South Korea had strategic economic reasons to push the shipbuilding industry, and they offered incentives to the relatively small shipbuilders in the country. But this came at a time when the world didn't need many new ships. Existing ship orders were being cancelled all over the world.

The Koreans went after existing orders. They tried to set up meetings with the few who were placing orders. With no significant experience or expertise, most of the time, they were politely asked to leave. A few times, they managed to secure a meeting. Then they'd be asked, 'You don't have any experience, nor are you experts, why should we place an order with you?' The South Koreans would reply, 'We'll do it for very cheap.' 'Yes, but your competitors are experienced and cheap also.'

In their desperate negotiations, some of these Korean companies' officials without even looking at the requirements would simply ask the other side, 'How much are they building your ship for? We'll build it for less than that.' The Koreans, at that point, didn't have much to offer. They had one thing the others didn't – cheap labour. Globally, shipbuilding companies were in distress. The Koreans started hiring engineers from companies in Western Europe and Japan. Eventually, the ball was set rolling.

The Koreans didn't have any experience designing ships. So they bought licences for existing designs from consulting companies. About a decade later, their order books were active. Towards the start of the 1980s, they built massive yards to construct the ships. To give you a sense of scale, one of the ships built had a deck space twice the size of a football field. The yard they have to build such ships is the size of 700 football fields. And this is just one yard. At every stage, there were problems. At one such stage, the problem was that there weren't enough trained engineers. They could only hire so many European engineers. They started to address this problem and began to train and up-skill existing workers.

In the mid-1980s, they started making more of their own equipment used in shipbuilding as opposed to importing everything. Gradually, they started designing their own ships instead of buying licences for existing designs. Towards the 1990s, these Korean companies were making very large ships – the biggest in the world. By the 2000s, they weren't just using and incorporating existing technology, they were inventing technology that didn't exist.

As you might have guessed, this translates well to the world of investing also. What the Korean companies did was start with whatever they knew how to do. In investing, you cannot wait to learn and then start for that never works. You either never start or never actually learn. What you should do is start without making giant mistakes. There were companies that perished because they took too many big risks. And then, as you gain skill and confidence, you improve your game.

If at the start the Korean companies had set out to build the biggest and most technologically advanced ship, they'd have failed. But today, they do just that. Back in the 1970s, less than 1 per cent of the global ship market was served by a South Korean company. By the 1990s, this number was 25 per cent.

Today? Today, if you see a ship with a deck size comparable to a football field and an engine bigger than most four-storey apartment buildings, chances are, somewhere inside the ship, there's a badge that says, 'Made in South Korea'.

25

Why Do Stocks Go Up?

IF YOU READ EUROPEAN history, you'll come across phrases like XYZ person 'discovered' India or America or some far-off land. What's there to discover? Weren't people living in India or America before the Europeans came? They were, but their history is written from a European perspective and until a few centuries ago, they didn't really know much about the world beyond Europe. And then they started making sea voyages about five centuries ago.

They travelled to far-flung areas (like India) and discovered 'new land'. They brought home (to Europe) resources from these new countries. At that point in time, the supply of novel things seemed endless. They discovered spices, different foods, tools and techniques and much more. These brave people, who spent years travelling to and from, started becoming incredibly wealthy. The wealth was so enticing, most were ready to overlook the dangers of these journeys – storms at sea, attacks by pirates and hostility from people at the destination. More entrepreneurs dipped their toes – they bought ships, supplies and labour with borrowed money and set off.

These entrepreneurs soon realised that the opportunity was so massive, there wasn't one person who could individually carry out such large-scale voyages. Collectively, a new company was created – the Dutch East India Company. The amount of money this company needed was so large that the existing lenders were insufficient. They decided to tap into the power of public money. They offered part ownership of the company to the general public – whoever wanted to buy. What would they get in return? Would the money be paid back? All you got was ownership of a small part of the company. And as an owner, you'd be entitled to whatever profits the company made.

If all the ships of the Dutch East India Company sank in the ocean, nobody would come to give you money. If they made a profit, you were entitled to the profits proportional to the amount of the company you owned. This is also known as dividends. This way, the Dutch East India Company was able to raise money for their massive voyages. Thankfully for the public, the company made massive profits – profits that were shared with them. Seeing this, people who didn't own any shares in the company wanted to own some.

The piece of paper that was proof of ownership of shares – that was something you could sell and buy. So, you could trade shares of the company. If you were the owner of a share and wanted money for some other purpose, or thought you could make more money elsewhere, you could sell the shares and get money for them. There were designated meeting spots where sellers and buyers would come to find each other. These were called exchanges. So that is essentially how we have reached where we are today.

Today, exchanges are computerised and trades happen in milliseconds. It gets complicated after this. But all the ways of making money from stocks start with this – profits. Today, you will hear phrases like intraday trading, high-frequency trading and growth investing.

Many of these investors don't really care about the profits a company makes. What they care about is how they can sell at a higher price. And eventually, every 'higher price' is justified only by the profits a company makes. There are many companies that won't share profits with you – for now. They keep the profits to fund the future growth of the company. No matter the type of investing, they depend on the dividend. If they don't depend on the dividend, then they depend on someone else paying a higher price for the stock – which eventually depends on the earnings or profits or dividends. It's all about the profits.

26

What Are Others Doing?

INDIAN TRUCKS ARE VERY different from the ones found in Europe or the US. Truckers all over the world love to take care of their trucks. In the West, it is common for truckers to polish their trucks' paint to match expensive luxury limousines.

In India, truckers don't care much about polish, but they love painting caricatures, phrases and the Indian flag. Truckers worldwide use radium tape. Radium tape (usually red, yellow or white) is a tape that glows in the dark if a slight amount of light falls on it. Large vehicles put these tapes in straight lines on the sides of their vehicles. This makes the size of the vehicle easier to acknowledge for others on the road and increases safety for all.

About two decades ago, a few Indian truckers discovered that they could make very creative use of radium tape. Besides just having it stretched along the sides, they started cutting and making art from these radium tapes. If you go on any highway in India, you will notice that almost all trucks have radium tape on their sides for safety. And most trucks will have radium tape used for creative truck art on the front, side, back and even underneath.

What is happening here is very quintessentially human. Imitation. Humans imitate. We learn by copying others, mostly from someone we think is better than us. In Europe, smokers held their cigarettes between their thumbs and index fingers. Hollywood movies popularised holding the cigarette between the index finger and the middle finger. Now nearly everybody holds it the way Hollywood taught them — because movie stars are imitated.

But imitation also has its flaws. In the 1960s, a prestigious school called Lakeside School in the US installed something almost no other school in the world had: a computer. Most students were not able to do much with it. One thirteen-year-old boy was awed by it and he and a friend skipped classes to work on it. They tried and tested it to understand how it functioned and eventually got extremely good at it.

By the time the boy was sixteen years old, he had sold software to measure traffic in his area. His father was a lawyer, and he pressured him to prepare for law. The boy went to Harvard University. In the midst of that, he falsely persuaded a computer company, telling them that he'd written a code they wanted. In the few days before he met them, he actually wrote the code, and it worked. He dropped out of Harvard and started his own company. This boy's name was Bill Gates, founder of Microsoft.

This story is what we all hear: he dropped out of Harvard. But what they don't talk about is that almost nobody in the world had access to a computer at the age of thirteen. Only some kids had access through their expensive, prestigious schools. Bill Gates might have left Harvard, but he came from a wealthy family — his father was a well-to-do lawyer. When you factor in those parts of the story, you realise he had an unfair advantage. This is not to say Bill Gates wasn't capable. His capability, nobody doubts.

Successful people can have many unfair disadvantages too — no denying that. But imagine being thirteen years old in the 1960s. If you had imitated him and dropped out of college to start a computer business, what are the odds you'd succeed? When you're investing, don't just copy what others are doing. Additionally, don't just copy what famous people seem to be doing. You don't know the path they took. You don't know if they had any unfair advantages.

Look at yourself. Look at the advantages you have. Use your advantages. Understand if you have the same advantage as someone else who's done well. But don't make decisions based on someone else's moves. You might not know what advantages they've had.

27

If Not This, Then That

You would have heard these names – Walmart or Costco. In the US, they sell everything you could need on a daily basis. They're masters at what they do. They have massive warehouse-sized centres where people go shopping. But their true strength lies in their supply chain management.

Orders are placed in advance by predicting how much their customers will buy. Some things are seasonal like Christmas trees, some come under daily needs like milk and vegetables, some are durable like cutlery. They can store a pack of plastic spoons for years even if nobody buys it but can store fresh apples for a few days and fresh milk for an even shorter period. In January 2020, most of these stores had cleared out Christmas-related items. Most items had been sold. A few that were left behind were either thrown away or kept for the next year, depending on how perishable the item was.

The US shot a missile targeting an Iranian military person.[1] Tensions were high. Some feared this could be the start of the Third World War. In India, the markets had touched a new high – a relief to investors after the nervous year 2019 with its ups and downs. In China, everybody was talking about a mysterious new virus spreading on the streets of Wuhan.[2]

China started imposing strict lockdowns. Production of goods and items in the country – also known as the factory of the world – slowed down and even stopped. Some auto parts started facing a crunch. Gadget factories too started faltering. February came and went. Not much had changed. Most of the world was functioning as it already did. Parts of China started emerging out of lockdowns. Many around the world were now talking about what was happening in China. Everyone was still treating this virus as someone else's problem.

Still, the world carried on. There were a few sparse cases of the virus appearing in different parts of the world, but Italy and Iran rang the bells in desperation. Suddenly, a greater number of people around the world sat up and stared at their screens. This was proof that this virus wasn't going to be only China's problem. As soon as March arrived, flights started to get shut down. Governments all over the world started carrying out tests. Some asked the unthinkable – is this going to be a global pandemic? The public started showing initial signs of panic all around the world.

Experts warned of an economic crisis. They warned of many other things too like power grid failure, food shortages and mass illnesses. The supply chain experts at Walmart, Costco and other major stores were listening. They were smart and always kept an eye out for what could be in demand. People with the power to act were sure something big was coming and they would have to prepare for it.

Whatever was thought to be most in demand was ordered extra: milk, vegetables and meat. Then they thought of the next layer of items like snacks and long-lasting edible products. Next came sanitisers, detergents and soaps. Store shelves were stacked with additional items. And then, the lockdowns struck.

People rushed to stores to fill up their carts with what they thought they would need for at least the next three

FIGURE 27.1 People stocking toilet paper during the COVID-19 pandemic

months. Who knew when the next batch of items would arrive in stores again? The first thing to run out of stock was ... toilet paper.[3] Who would have thought? You'd imagine people would prioritise buying food over storing toilet paper, but no, toilet paper ran out.

Pictures circulated online of stores with shelves filled with food and milk beside empty shelves where toilet paper was supposed to be stacked. Nobody had thought this would happen. There were no additional stocks. The toilet paper shelves in stores remained empty for weeks. Why did this happen though? This was an unexpected consequence of the pandemic. The obvious ones, we all tried to prepare for. The not-so-obvious ones, we find very hard to prepare for.

When you're investing, remember, you're dealing with this exact world. The same world that bought more toilet paper than food. There are going to be unexpected consequences. When you take a quick bet, remember, no matter how easy and obvious a bet seems, this world can surprise you.

News channels just announced that the monsoon is going to be great for a particular year. Will fertiliser stocks go up? They usually do. Yes, chances are they might. And if some random incident plays out, the opposite might happen too. How that would happen, we don't know. (But you'll find enough people to explain how that would happen after it has happened). We love a simple cause-and-effect story. What this example aims to tell you is that even a system of cause and effect, if complex enough, can surprise you in both pleasant and unpleasant ways.

The world doesn't work with simple cause-and-effect relations. The same cause and effect can produce different results each time – this is termed probability. This can also be very rewarding. It is important to plan in a manner that, no matter the outcome, you don't lose all you have. Additionally, plan in a way that, if the outcome is good, your gains increase exponentially.

28

Which Strategy You Adopt

In the 1950s, the Korean War was in full swing. The North Koreans had taken over South Korea and the US wanted to help the South Koreans fight back. This was just after the Second World War. The US was still in control of Japan and they urged the Japanese to fulfil an urgent requirement. They needed small off-road SUVs.

Toyota stepped in and made a vehicle that looked oddly like the Willys MB Jeep used by the American troops in the Second World War. These vehicles were absolutely dependable.

FIGURE 28.1 Willys MB Jeep used during the Second World War

Once the war was over, Toyota realised they had a good product on their hands. They started selling these cars to civilians too. In comparison to the others in the same range, Toyota's car didn't have much to offer — it was very bare and utilitarian. But it had one very crucial thing going for it — it was reliable. This meant that people who truly depended on cars, mostly farmers, loved these Toyotas.

Over the years, gradually, these cars evolved and became better with each generation. More people started buying them. Just as gradually, luxurious items like air-conditioning and music systems were added. With the adoption of this vehicle by families, the company named it the Toyota Land Cruiser. Similarly, Toyota also launched a pickup truck called the Hilux.

One peculiarity was that the Toyotas weren't always equipped with the latest technology in automobiles. They had a habit of holding onto technology that was time-proven. But buyers who bought these Toyotas mostly overlooked the technology bit because these SUVs and pickup trucks were practically indestructible. Both were sold all over the world – Australia, Asia, Africa and America.

FIGURE 28.2 Toyota Land Cruiser

Everywhere, the owners said one thing: the durability of these vehicles was unmatched. They just don't go bad! Their reliability was extraordinary. There are stories of owners who 'forgot' to get the engine oil serviced in their cars for years, and the cars still worked. A video from the TV show, *Top Gear*, shows the Toyota Hilux getting submerged in the ocean, dropped from a great height and much more.[1] After all that, it still switched on.

Look at documentaries of places that have incredibly tough terrain – the Middle East, Africa, Southeast Asia and Australia. It could be a documentary about anything – photography, wildlife, society, protests or movements. More often than not the vehicles used would be a Toyota truck or SUV.

The United Nations sends aid to regions torn by civil war, and they don't use Jeeps or Range Rovers. They use Toyota Land Cruisers. There are good off-road vehicles like the Jeep and Range Rover that can take you to places where roads are a distant dream, and so can the Toyota. But none can offer the dependable reliability that a Toyota can. This philosophy trickles down to Toyota's other cars too.

There's a reason why cab operators love the Etios and the Innova: Toyota only uses technology that it knows will work. Toyota doesn't send out cars with new technology until it is sure it works. This also means that some of these technologies take longer to appear in Toyota cars compared to their availability in other cars.

When you add something new and complicated, there's a chance something might go wrong. The more complicated something is, the more the chance of something going wrong. Human nature is such, if you spend enough time and effort, complicated things become simpler. When we were little toddlers, reading a five-letter word like 'apple' required effort. Now, we can finish thick books in a matter of hours.

Toyota adds to its cars what it thinks is simple. And for it to think something is simple, it needs to have mastered it. This is why any new technology is first available in other cars but takes time to show up on a Toyota SUV or pickup truck. Toyota would rather skip the latest trendy technology than add something unproven.

If you're new to investing, there will be many strategies and ideas that appeal to you. They might all be great strategies. They might work very well for many people. But do you know those strategies enough to use them? Are those strategies simple to you? Because if they're not, you're not going to be able to use them even if they work.

With your investment, be exactly like Toyota. You are Toyota and your investments are Toyota Hilux. It's your most prized possession. Make sure you thoroughly understand what you're doing with your investments. If some new investment or strategy or stock or mutual fund or asset attracts your attention, make sure you understand it enough before making it a part of your investment.

Never heard of the name Toyota Hilux? In India, we don't have such a big market for pickup trucks. But Toyota does sell it in India – sort of. Based on the Hilux pickup truck, Toyota developed an SUV that they sell in India – the Toyota Fortuner.

29

Look Left and Right to Cross the Road

DIET IS CRUCIAL. WHAT you eat is what you are (or what you aren't). Naturally, many of us are careful with our diet. Kuntal Joisher, a mountaineer based out of Mumbai, had climbed some of the toughest-to-climb mountains in the world by 2014. In 2014, he decided to climb the world's tallest mountain – Mount Everest.

Everest Base Camp, a point from where mountaineers start off on the arduous journey to the summit, is where all climbers reach and rest. After spending time there to acclimatise, climbers set off on the journey to the top. Sherpas – a local ethnic group in Nepal – are extremely adept in the tough region. It is a standard practice for any mountaineer to take Sherpas as their guide to the top. The Sherpas know the region better than any mountaineer, however, they themselves are not immune to the treacherous conditions of the region.

In 2014, while Kuntal was at the Everest Base Camp in Nepal, right before he set off for this journey, a massive avalanche struck, and sixteen Sherpas died.[1] The plan was cancelled. Kuntal returned the next year. This time, an earthquake struck the region. Again, there were avalanches. Kuntal barely managed to escape.

The climb to Mount Everest is infamous for being extremely treacherous. There have been several who have died attempting the climb. Even today, every now and then, mountaineers do die attempting the climb.

The reason could be anything ranging from adverse weather conditions, natural disasters like avalanches, running out of oxygen or food, or simply an individual's exhaustion. A good way to understand how tough this is is to watch the 2015 movie *Everest*. The entire trail of the mountain is littered with used oxygen cylinders, tents, climbing gear and dead bodies. At those temperatures, decomposition is impossible. Mountaineers who died decades ago still look as though they died yesterday.

In 2016, Kuntal went to the base camp again to attempt the climb. He braved the nightmarish winds and sub-zero temperature, ate snacks that he carried with him and hoped for the best. He spent four days climbing and finally reached the top where he spent twenty minutes admiring the view. According to him, those minutes were so unforgettable and could only be compared to the birth of his daughter.

He used his satellite phone to call home after which he began his descent. The descent also takes a long time and several climbers have died on their way back. Thankfully, Kuntal made it home safely. By the time he returned, he was famous. He wasn't just famous in Mumbai; he was famous world wide. Newspapers all over the world had mentioned him.

Scores of people climb Mount Everest every year – many of them are Indian. What made Kuntal so different that the world was talking about him? Kuntal was the first vegan in the world to climb Mount Everest.[2] Veganism is focused on consuming only non-animal products. It is different from vegetarianism. Vegetarians stay away from meat but consume milk and other dairy products. Vegans don't consume even dairy products because they believe it is unfair and cruel to animals.

When you're climbing that high up, you need calories, protein, calcium and vitamins. Climbers argue that without consuming dairy and meat products, it is impossible to make the climb. He proved them wrong. Vegans the world over argue that a plant-based vegan diet is sufficient in every way for us. Vegans go on to claim that a meat- and dairy-free diet has incredible benefits – lower chances of diabetes, lowered cholesterol, lower obesity, better sleep and more.

Veganism as a movement has caught on in the world and has many famous proponents. On the other end of the spectrum, you have believers of the carnivore diet. Again, these people are different from non-vegetarians. Non-vegetarians eat meats, eggs, vegetables, fruits, and consume dairy products. Those who follow the carnivore diet eat only meat – no vegetables, no fruits. As you'd imagine, vegans and carnivore dieters don't get along that well with each other.

Some very famous people have adopted the carnivore diet and spoken of incredible benefits – more energy, lowered cholesterol, lowered stress and some have even said it cured their depression. See what's happening? Both extremes – vegans and carnivore-diet eaters – claim similar benefits. What's happening? Why can't both sides sit down, read what science says, and conclude what is actually good for the human body? Then there'd be no debate. We would all know what's good for us.

Here's where it gets funny. Both sides claim to study science and have science-backed research to suggest they're correct. The world of food and nutrition is filled with abundant research. Food and nutrition are a complicated space and it is not necessary that what works for one person will work the same for the other. If you look hard enough, you'll find something that agrees with your opinion. This is exactly what both sides are doing.

The vegans look for research that suggests their diet style is optimal, and they find exactly that. The carnivore-diet eaters look for research that suggests their diet style is optimal, and they too find exactly that. Vegans and carnivore dieters don't look for research that might suggest their diet is poor. This is called confirmation bias.

When we believe something, we look for information that agrees with us. We never look for information that might disprove our beliefs. This is prevalent in almost every human on earth. Be it politics, scientific beliefs, technological beliefs or even investments, we look to confirm what we like. This can turn out extremely sourly for your investments.

If you like a stock, mutual fund or any asset, don't just look for reasons that support your argument. Look for reasons that disprove your belief too. When you have both sides, compare them. Only then will you get an accurate picture and know how the pros weigh against the cons. Otherwise, it's like crossing the road looking only to the right and not the left. You need to check both left and right.

What kind of diet is truly correct for us? Proponents of all kinds of diets need to get rid of their confirmation bias. Maybe then, we'll get to the bottom of this. Some of the societies where people live the longest – Okinawa in Japan or the Mediterranean region – what kind of diet do you think they follow? This doesn't prove anything, but they follow neither of the two diets. They have a little bit of everything.

30

Only Correct Information Is Useful

In the late 1930s, much of Southeast Asia was a European colony. The modern-day country of the Philippines was controlled by the US. This period in world history is extremely dark. To truly understand why, one needs to investigate further back in history. We won't be doing that here. We'll simply take it from a certain point in time because we have a specific lesson to learn from it. So, back to the late 1930s. The US and Japan were at war with each other. In an effort to intimidate the US, Japan started advancing and capturing territory in Southeast Asia by directly fighting the European settlements. In response, the US put trade embargoes on Japan and cut off their crude oil supply among other items.

The hope was that this move would weaken Japan as the country was small in size. It lacked many resources like crude oil and raw materials for metals. Japan had enough reserves for two years but after that, they would run out. They made a bold decision to capture big chunks of Southeast Asia from the Europeans and the Philippines from the Americans. The Japanese wanted supremacy over the Pacific region.

This entire region would be enough for Japan to secure its resources and serve as a major stronghold for the Japanese – something to deter the Americans and the Europeans. During this period, the US had one primary enemy – Germany. It was focusing on that conflict in Europe. Japan succeeded in its plan. Pumped and motivated by this, the Japanese wanted to send another strong message to the

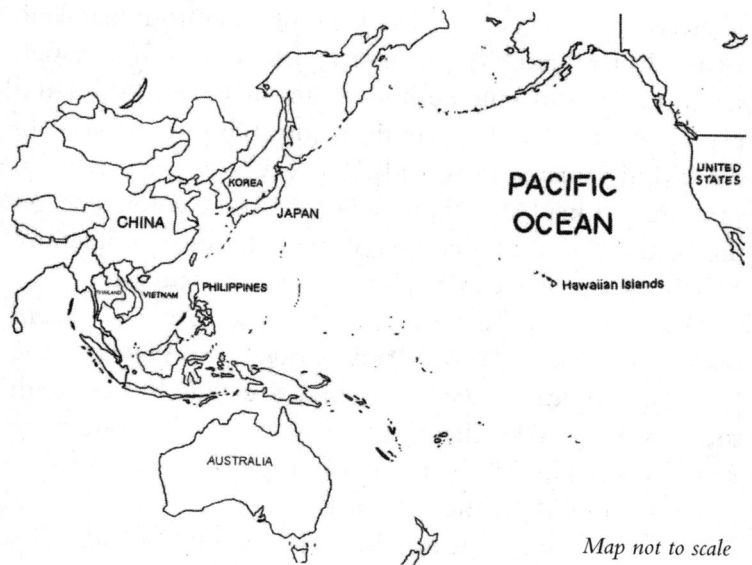

FIGURE 30.1 Areas Japan wished to control for their resources

US – one it hoped would keep the US scared and away from the Pacific for long.

In Pearl Harbor, several American warships and aircraft were stationed. In 1941, the Japanese attacked this site. Hundreds of warplanes were lost and ships were sunk. Most American sailors at Pearl Harbor died – over 2,000 of them. It was an extremely well-coordinated move on Japan's part. It succeeded in damaging the resources and morale of the Americans – though only temporarily. Towards 1943, America began to push back.

Gradually, the American forces were able to regain land that had been taken over by the Japanese. The Japanese held honour in great regard. Many soldiers would kill themselves to avoid being captured and imprisoned. The losses, however, of both life and resources were immense on both sides. There was no one side that was clearly better than the other. The bloodshed continued into the mid-1940s.

Japan had been cornered and was fighting from mainland Japan. But it did not surrender. Japan was in a tough situation – it had suffered huge losses of soldiers, ships and planes. All this while its trade connectivity to the rest of the world remained suspended. The US wanted Japan to surrender. It kept air-dropping bombs in the country to get the Japanese to surrender, finally giving Japan an ultimatum. When asked, the Japanese premier said, 'Mokusatsu.'

Mokusatsu in Japanese literally translates to 'silent contempt'. The US had had enough. Seeing that the Japanese wouldn't surrender, the US decided to go with the option it had threatened to go with – complete destruction. The US had started a top-secret new project in 1941 – the Manhattan Project.

In 1945, after hearing the premier say 'mokusatsu', America decided to use what it had developed during the Manhattan Project – the nuclear bomb. On 6 August 1945, a Boeing B-29 bomber plane named 'Enola Gay' dropped the first-ever nuclear bomb to be used in a war on the city of Hiroshima. Three days later, another nuclear bomb was dropped on the city of Nagasaki.

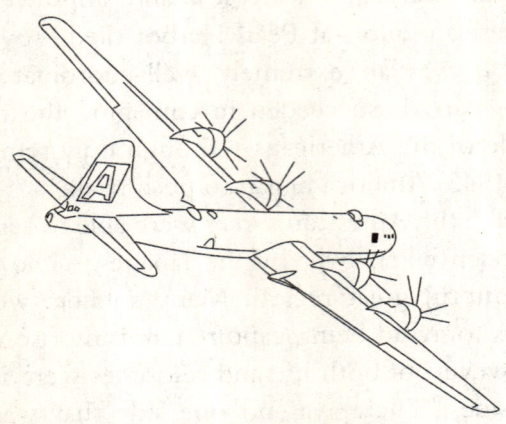

FIGURE 30.2 Boeing B-29 bomber plane that dropped the first nuclear bomb on Hiroshima in 1945

The cities were destroyed. Lakhs of citizens died. Japan surrendered. Those were the only two times anyone has ever used a nuclear bomb in a war. Numerous lives were lost over the years – Japanese, American and others.

This isn't about which side was right or which was wrong. That's a debate for another day. Here's something chilling: the Japanese premier said 'mokusatsu' which means 'silent contempt'. The translator to the Americans translated this as just that – silent killing. However, 'mokusatsu' in Japan is also used to mean 'no comments'.

The Japanese premier didn't say he wanted to continue fighting the Americans. He was avoiding commenting on the situation – probably trying to delay the decision to a later point in time. It was a giant miscommunication, a miscommunication that if it hadn't happened, could have saved the lives of countless innocent civilians.

We're living in an information age where fake news and misunderstandings are common. Before taking any major decision, be it an investment decision or otherwise, make sure your source of information and its interpretation are correct. Several investors have lost money to murmurs that amounted to nothing in reality or because they interpreted correct information in the wrong way. Everyone is trying to obtain more information. Not many are trying to ensure the information is correct; do that.

31

Whom Not to Take Advice From

In 1882, a boy named Charles was born in Lugo, Italy. His family was not wealthy and was going through a rough phase. But Charles always liked money. He moved to Rome to study at a university there, but he never did well — something he himself admitted.

While in university, he spent most of his time in bars and cafes with his rich friends. At that time, Italians were migrating to the US in search of economic opportunities and Charles jumped on a ship too. On reaching the US, he looked for odd jobs in the city of Boston. He worked as a dishwasher, waiter, busboy and several other jobs but he could not keep them for a long duration.

Charles then moved to the city of Montreal in Canada where he found a new opportunity — one that he hoped would allow him to get rich. The new job he got was that of a bank teller. Charles was a suave man. He was charismatic, spoke three languages (English, Italian and French) and people enjoyed his company. He quickly rose through the ranks at the bank. The bank he was working at offered a very high interest rate to its customers. More and more depositors invested.

But unknown to the customers, the owner of the bank was paying off earlier investors with money gotten from new investors. This was only going to last so long. One sudden day, the owner of the bank fled with the money to Mexico, leaving the investors with no money. Charles was empty-handed too. Desperate for money, he forged a cheque and got caught and was sent to prison for three years.

After that, Charles returned to Boston. Here, he found another trade that he hoped would earn him big money. He started trafficking migrants from Italy illegally. He was caught and sent to prison. After his release, he tried to live a life away from trouble.

Charles fell in love with a woman, got married and worked as a bank teller. He quit and took over his father-in-law's fruit business. Then he moved on from that because none of the roles really worked for him. It was at this point that he discovered the International Reply Coupon (IRC). IRCs are postal stamps accepted internationally and they cost the same everywhere. However, due to different inflation rates in different countries, you could buy them cheaper from some countries and sell them at a higher rate elsewhere. This was an arbitrage opportunity.

FIGURE 31.1 Charles Ponzi

Charles got into this business. He used his money and made good returns. He tried to borrow money from banks so he could make even more money, but they flat-out refused. So he collected some money from his friends and family. To them, he promised extremely high returns – double in ninety days – and they agreed.

Before Charles could reach the end of the ninety-day period, some more people heard of it and asked him to take their money, which he did.

Using the freshly collected money, he paid back the first few investors. Now, you had a bunch of investors who had been paid back – people who had actually made money from Charles's scheme. He was very smart about his offers. He never pushed people.

The way it would work is, he would make a casual mention of the work he did in conversations. If someone was interested, they'd ask him for more information. If they didn't, he left it there and didn't try to bring it up again. To those who did enquire more, he would explain 'IRCs' patiently.

Here is the thing about knowledge. If you don't know anything about a domain, anybody speaking confidently to you will sound like an expert. Most people had no information on how these stamps' arbitrage opportunities worked and so they believed him.

Charles wouldn't just take someone's money. He'd usually accept only if they really requested and pleaded with him. His sophisticated mannerisms, charismatic personality and seemingly good knowledge won him the trust of investors. There's a famous scene in the movie *American Hustle* that seems like the exact representation of this. At this point, he's not making money from the stamps. He's just taking money from new investors and giving it to older ones.

Since Charles promised such high returns, he needed more new investors than the last round. This, thankfully for Charles, wasn't a problem. Word kept spreading and more investors started giving him money. At the height of his fame, he was earning $250,000 a day in 1920!

A newspaper covered him, and all hell broke loose – people lined up outside his house to invest. He bought a palatial house and a beautiful limousine – true to his lavish style. His arrogance had reached such a peak that he bought one of the banks that had refused to give him a loan. He even bought another company just to be able to fire his ex-boss. People would ask around about how these things work. Nobody knew how it worked.

But a few of the early investors had made money so they served as social proof. Humans are social animals, and they fell for it. Eventually, it blew up – there is no other way these things can go – and he was sent to prison. Investors lost 70 per cent of their investment.

Charles came out after six years. His name was tarnished in Boston, so he went to Florida to start a fresh new life. There he started a real estate business and started selling land. Most of this land was underwater – in the swamps. Investors, just like before, had fallen for his tactics again. He was caught again and imprisoned. When he came out of prison, he was deported to Italy. There too he started a few scams, fled to Brazil and died of old age in Rio de Janeiro. He had only enough money to cover his funeral.

Now, this is always going to be a tricky matter. New investment opportunities arise once in a while and people have to depend on someone else's expertise to make decisions. What's the way out? How can we choose someone to advise us correctly? For most things, a reasonable level of knowledge should be developed in each of us. You might not be a doctor, but if a fake doctor

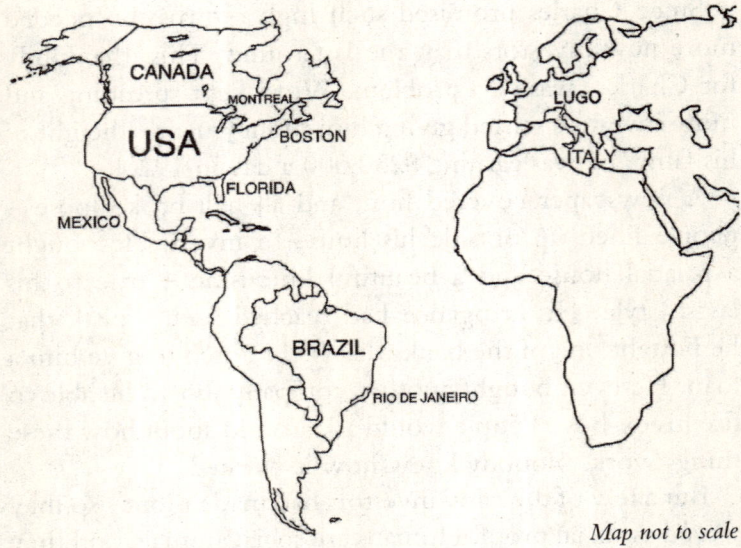

FIGURE 31.2 Cities Charles Ponzi travelled

told you that your fifth kidney has a stone in it, you'd know they're lying – we have only two kidneys.

Similarly, most of us cannot be full-time finance professionals. But most of us can have a basic level of knowledge and understanding so that it is more difficult to be cheated. With vital money matters, it makes sense to develop a baseline level of knowledge – just as many of us do with matters of our health.

There can be new forms of investment or niches within existing investments that we know nothing about. What about those? What can we do then? In those cases, you must remember, when things seem to be too good, they might just be too good. If you must take advice, make sure it isn't from someone who is also trying to sell you the investment.

There are some red flags that should definitely keep you on alert: high returns promised with low risk, investments in unregulated spaces where there is little legal protection, guaranteed returns and short periods where the window to invest vanishes very fast. Depending on the situation, there can be more red flags. Analyse carefully whenever you're investing.

A missed investment opportunity is better than money lost forever. What Charles did – collecting more money from investors to pay earlier investors – is a scam. It has to blow up. This is called a Ponzi scheme and is named after Charles himself. His full name was Charles Ponzi. He succeeded because he was the sole expert and advisor in whatever investments he sold.

32

What Happened in 2008

You want to buy a house. You take a loan from the bank. The bank asks you, 'What if you don't pay back?' You say, 'Take my home and sell it.' That makes sense. The bank gives you a loan and in case you don't pay, the bank will take over your house and sell it and recover its money. That's collateral.

Banks also lend money to big corporations and don't always have collateral. So a loan where the bank has collateral is considered safer for the bank. In the early 2000s, the banks in the US were giving out loans to people for buying houses. The economy had just recovered from the technology bubble in 2000 where many banks had given out loans to businesses that had shut down. Against this backdrop, the banks found giving home loans safer.

At the same time, real estate prices were climbing steadily. The banks weren't as worried about the loans since they thought they could always sell the house and recover their money – probably even more than they were supposed to get. Banks can sell loans to other institutions. When they do so, the money need not be paid back to the original bank but to the new owner of the loans (or mortgage). They did so.

Investors loved the idea of a safe loan that was backed by collateral. This created great demand for buying mortgages from banks. Banks made good money by selling these loans. There was a demand for them, and they started giving out even more loans to supply the high demand. In doing so, they started giving loans to people who weren't as creditworthy (people who weren't as likely to pay back).

Nobody was too concerned about this because they thought that if these low creditworthy borrowers didn't pay back, the bank could always take over their property and sell it to recover the money. Here's what was happening at this point: banks give out money to borrowers to buy a house, then they sell this mortgage to institutional investors, so they again have money. The banks lend this money again and sell this new mortgage to institutional investors. This cycle continues.

But towards the end of 2007, many people start defaulting on their loans. No big deal. The mortgage owners can sell the houses and recover their money. They start putting these houses up for sale. More people default on their loans, resulting in more houses on sale. Here's where it becomes bad. Supply and demand kick in. There are so many houses on sale and not enough buyers which leads to a fall in the prices of the listed houses.

Suddenly, mortgage owners realise they can't recover their money. More borrowers start defaulting on their loans resulting in more houses getting listed for sale. As houses continue to become cheaper, borrowers cannot recover their money and banks run out of money to lend. Without money to lend, other industries that rely on loans to operate (like the auto and construction industries) cannot operate. With some industries slowing down, the economic cycle starts getting affected. One industry affects the other and soon, most industries are down and suffering. This further leads to job losses and reduced spending. As a result, with reduced spending comes a slowdown.

This is the extremely simplified story of how the 2008 recession – also called the Great Recession – happened. Right after the 2000 technology bubble, investors and the entire economic system was determined to avoid another technology bubble. In doing so, they let the housing bubble build and finally burst in 2008. The US was such a major economy that this recession hit worldwide. The US Fed printed money and managed to stimulate the economy back to health over the next few years. The impact of such massive events is that people's focus is on making sure the same doesn't repeat.

From 2012 and 2013, every few months you would hear someone talking about the impending recession or bubble. That continued right from 2012 to 2020. In 2020, the markets fell just as sharply. But this 2020 market crash was not caused by a housing bubble or tech bubble. It was caused by a pandemic – a threat nobody saw coming.

The next recession, whenever it comes, hopefully, will be much farther away and milder in nature, and will probably not be caused by a housing bubble or a virus. It will be caused by something that the markets, by and large, aren't prepared for or cautious about.

The lesson for the investor is the same – be it the technology bubble of 2000, the Great Recession of 2008 or the pandemic of 2020. Make sure you have enough emergency money kept safely, invest in a diversified manner to stay safe from sudden shocks and always keep a safety margin in your investments. Another important control every investor needs to have is control over their own fear and greed. Don't get too greedy when the markets are good. Don't be too fearful when the markets are bad. Recessions have been different each time. But the same investment strategy has done well through all those recessions.

33

IPO Frenzy of the Late 1990s

In the late 1990s, there were several IPOs (in the US) that altered how investors viewed stocks. Not just stocks, it changed what people thought a successful business looked like. There was an e-commerce company. You might be making guesses as to where this is going.

A successful business was one that was making profits. This was the only requirement – up until now. This was followed by a slew of technology companies that had a dot-com at the end of their name. One of these was an e-commerce company. It had operations in California and was looking to expand its warehouses all over the US, and therefore, it needed the money from the IPO.

Sceptics worried if the smaller size of the orders would make economic sense for the company to deliver. Some were sure it would work, and that the scepticism was a result of people not understanding how the internet worked. The company's IPO launched. And then the stock was listed on Nasdaq. It climbed. But the company kept facing troubles.

The company was expanding very rapidly and that came with its own set of problems. The delivery infrastructure wasn't in place and was often flawed. It made desperate attempts by buying new delivery vehicles and renting warehouses to solve the delivery problem. This new frontier was so unheard of that legacy investor Warren Buffett had stayed away from this space. Very few understood the internet, and those who did thought it was the future. They invested accordingly.

In 2001, this company declared bankruptcy. This is Webvan. Without names being mentioned it sounds oddly like the Amazon stock. The difference between the two was that Amazon survived. Not just survived, it eventually thrived. If you had invested in XYZ IPO or stock twenty years ago, today you'd have … this is very easy to say.

Right now, there are multibagger stocks. Do you know which to buy? If you don't know now, how would you have known twenty years ago? In the late 1990s, there were several other dot-com stocks and IPOs. Many of them failed. Some succeeded. Amazon was one of them. Thousands of investors lost their money because they invested in dot-com stocks because they didn't understand it but thought it would do well. Those who understood it though, those investors made returns unheard of in decades.

Today, in India, we're entering a somewhat similar space. There are companies that haven't made a profit so far. We are not used to seeing such companies in the markets. Some of these companies will become large like Amazon. Some will go the Webvan way. Remember this when you consider applying for an IPO. It could be a bad investment or it could also be a great investment.

Don't fall for the hype and what others say. Do your research and if you don't understand, stay away from it. If you do understand, you might be on your way to bumper returns.

34

The Lesser-Known Tulip Tale

AROUND A 1,000 YEARS ago, a particular flower was becoming popular in Turkey. This flower was primarily found in Central Asia but not in Turkey. Its appearance was so unique and striking that it caught the attention of the royals of Turkey. Its name was derived from the Turkish word for turban, tülbend, and the flower was the tulip.

In the 1500s, the Sultan of Turkey fell deeply in love with the flower. He ordered that the flower be extensively cultivated to decorate his palace. In the early years of the 17th century, a botanist from the Netherlands travelled to Turkey. He was fascinated with the palace's obsession with the tulip flower. The flowers looked very beautiful, indeed. In the interest of science and research, he decided to carry a few tulip bulbs back home to the Netherlands.

Tulips are grown using tulip bulbs which are similar to potatoes. They grow as nodes in the roots of plants and can be planted separately yielding new tulip plants. Thus, the tulip flowers reached the Netherlands. Science might have been the original intention, but vanity caught on pretty fast. The tulip flowers became common in the wealthier households of the Netherlands.

Tulips don't grow very fast. The growth cycle of tulip bulbs spans years. It's not like you can plant one today and get a flower a week or a month later. As with anything that becomes popular among wealthy folk, other wealthy folk wanted tulips too. So whatever tulip bulbs were there in the market, their prices rose quite fast. As with cars, watches, handbags and other status symbols, people who weren't exactly wealthy but were a notch below wanted tulips too.

Here's where things change. So far, the price had been rising because more people wanted to buy the tulips and plant them. But since the prices of tulips rose so fast, it attracted the attention of people who weren't interested in the tulips themselves. It attracted people interested only in the rising price. Soon more people tried to buy tulip bulbs. Some bought the bulbs and sold them within a few days making huge gains. The news spread and more people bought the bulbs. Then, a new kind of tulip showed up.

Tulips usually are one solid colour. This new one had streaks. The news spread like wildfire. This even rarer tulip bulbs' prices rose to astronomical values. At one point, everybody wanted their hands on this tulip. The rich, the middle class, the poor – all poured vast amounts of their personal wealth into tulip bulbs.

Some very brave (or foolish) investors borrowed money to invest in tulips. It eventually reached a point where the sellers couldn't find buyers at the prices. Then the prices started to fall, and buyers kept lowering the offer price rapidly after that.

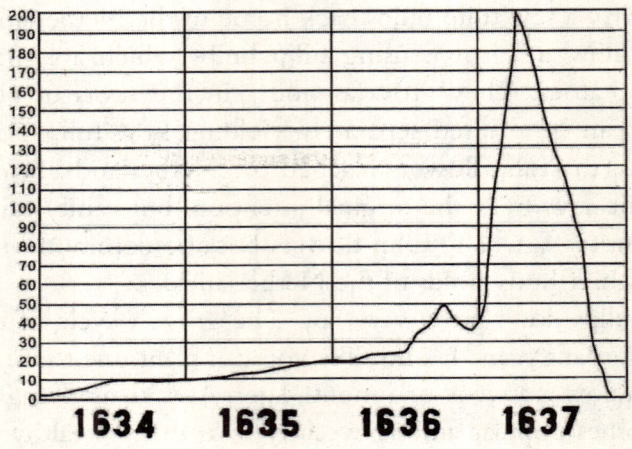

FIGURE 34.1 Index of tulips

The prices plummeted. The bubble had burst. Many people lost money. In the frenzy of watching prices rise multifold in a few days, people forgot to question what the tulips had to offer that justified prices like that. As an investor, this lesson is easy to listen to but may be difficult to adhere to.

This episode is called the Tulip Mania.[1] If you are not new to the world of personal finance, you would have heard of this tale a couple of times – it is a common example cited to caution investors from investing in manias. That's one lesson to take from this. There's another lesson.

Very often, in examples, Tulip Mania is believed by many to have ruined the economy of the Netherlands because so many had lost their money to this mania. The truth as we know now is that the Tulip Mania wasn't as big as some would like us to believe. It was a mania, no doubt. But it didn't affect the economy of the Netherlands in a monstrous manner.

The ultra-rare, streaked tulip bulbs were bought by fewer than 100 people. Another detail that is casually skipped while narrating this tale is that the reason the prices of tulips fell was the bubble bursting. Tulip supplies eventually caught up – so there were more tulip bulbs in the market suddenly in 1637. The streaked tulip wasn't a special tulip – it was caused by a viral infection that jumped to the tulips from potatoes.

There is information and then there is full information. That is the second, less popular lesson the Tulip Mania has to offer us. Today, the Netherlands is famous for its tulip fields – it is the world's largest producer of tulips. The Netherlands exports the flower all over the world. If you want a bouquet of tulips in India, you will have to pay around ₹800–₹1,000.

35

Which Game Are You Playing?

THE YEAR WAS 1847. A middle-aged man was stressed and restless in a hall of his house. In another room, his wife was about to give birth. This was his seventh child. The six children before had all died. A healthy little boy was born. The family was not extravagantly rich but was well-to-do.

The boy, who was the eldest child, grew up with his siblings who were well regarded by the neighbours who thought the siblings were all level-headed. Except for the one boy we're talking about – he was endlessly energetic and restless. They once found him sitting on duck eggs – trying to hatch them (he was unsuccessful). In school, he asked more questions than he answered, and the teachers complained about this habit to his mother.

Frustrated at the school's inability to satisfy the little boy's curiosity, the mother withdrew him from school and started teaching him at home. She encouraged him to read and write. And read, he did a lot. Eternally curious, he wanted to see more of the world. At the age of twelve, he left home to find a job. He got a job selling candy and newspapers on a train.

On the train, he convinced the conductor to let him run a little experiments lab in one corner. The twelve-year-old set up a chemistry lab in one corner of the luggage coach. He also made a printing press. Soon, he went from selling newspapers to printing his own newspaper on a train! It was a short newspaper but was well-received.

Four years after he joined the train, a random jerk caused some of his chemical jars to shatter. There was a small fire. It grew to become a big fire engulfing the entire coach. He was fired. As was always the case, this didn't affect his morale much. He found himself a job as a travelling telegrapher. The young boy continued to experiment and make things.

In 1869, he invented the universal stock ticker – his first big hit. A year later, he was able to sell it and take home a handsome income. He bought a house where he built a large lab – his dream lab. He put in the best equipment. He hired the best minds and then he got to work. He wanted to set up a lab that continually invented new things. Over the next few years, that is exactly what the lab did. Small but useful inventions kept pouring out of his lab.

In 1877 though, things changed. After tinkering with his lab mates, he invented a device that would speak! A device that would record human voices and talk back – the phonograph. This changed everything. He was called to the White House and everyone in America was talking about him. Singers, comedians, poets and musicians started recording themselves. This was the birth of recorded sound. Before this, if you wanted to listen to music, you had to listen to the artist live.

If you were an investor and were betting on this man's lab, you would be a very happy person. He was doing well all this while. But now, suddenly, he has done something so big that the world would never be the same again. Would you sell your shares now? If the question were asked in exactly this manner, your answer would probably be, 'No, I wouldn't selll.'

Why wouldn't you sell? This lab seems to have potential. It seems like this lab will produce more hits in the future.

However, countless investors sell their stocks the moment they see some upside. A stock doubled its value in one year's time. Would you sell? Or would you want to hold on? The logical answer seems to be to hold the stocks. But more investors sell after seeing some gains than holding on to a winner.

This man and his lab, just two years after inventing the phonograph, invented another world-changing invention. In fact, this invention was so massive, the habits of the world changed. The human sleep cycle changed. The invention: the light bulb. He didn't stop there. Another of his world-changing inventions was motion pictures. Before that, pictures were just still pictures. He invented video. He also worked on batteries. He worked on countless inventions and had 1,093 patents to his name. By now, it is obvious who this person is.

So why do people sell a winner much before the winner has won several games? This is because they imagine a different game. Horse racing. You are supposed to bet on horses. There are five horses running. You can bet on one. You bet on horse number three. It wins. Now, in the very next race, new horses are brought in. These horses, haven't raced today. Along with these fresh horses, the old winner (horse three) is also brought in. All other horses are rested and fresh. Only horse three is tired from the previous race. Will you bet on horse three this time?

When investors see a stock rise, they tend to think of it as a horse that has run its race. In investing, every single time, the question to ask really is: what kind of game is this? Is it a game where one round tires out your horse? Or is it a game where experience only helps with winning future games?

36

The Risk Nobody Prepared For

It is 3 a.m. Dark. Everybody is asleep. The beach, though, is anything but asleep. Groups of four to five men drag boats into the water. The water is rough, but they persist. Dragging the boats against the sand for a few metres, they continue to push the boats into the sea before jumping in and firing up the motors. In the pitch-black darkness, they continue to move without being able to see where they're headed. They use time to measure how far they have sailed. After a few hours, they push their nets into the sea. If luck favours them, they hit a patch where there are plenty of fish. After a few hours of this, they return to the mainland with what they've caught.

FIGURE 36.1 Boats being dragged to the sea by the fishermen

This description is not of one night only. It could easily describe any night over the last several decades in the southern coastal region of Tamil Nadu. For these fishermen, there are risks they have to prepare for. Some risks they can do something about. Others, they can do nothing about. There is a noteworthy custom among fishermen in these villages. On a day any fisherman dies, the entire village avoids going out to sea as a show of respect. Many modern-day customs in all societies across the globe actually have surprisingly practical origins. Besides respect, this also means that if the sea has bad weather, this custom prevents other fishermen from risking death. The fishermen, for this reason, have come to immensely respect the weather forecast office. The weather forecast for the immediate next few days is announced on the local radio. Some of them often choose to take additional risks by going out in bad weather too.

Over the last few decades though, there has been a new risk facing fishermen. Unlike the weather, this one is not a natural risk. It is a man-made risk. For centuries, fishermen in this region have fished these waters without any problem. Then, in 1976, a border was drawn on the map separating the sea into two sides – one that belonged to India and one that belonged to Sri Lanka.

There is no actual border marking in the water. Fishermen from both sides have to stay away from the general region if they want to stay away from the border. Those who do cross over are often arrested by the Sri Lankan Navy. Once caught, their boats are seized. Several have been arrested and imprisoned over the years. Often, the two governments strike agreements and the fishermen return home to India. But their boats do not come back. Even the smallest of boats can cost upwards of ₹20–₹30 lakh. Fishermen take loans to buy these boats. They then continue to service these loans for decades of their lives.

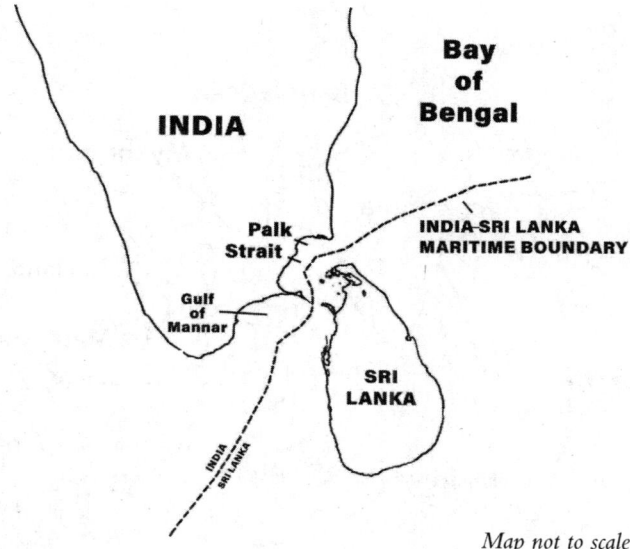

FIGURE 36.2 Border separating the sea into two sides

A fisherman in this region of India has to worry about so many risks – the weather, not catching enough fish, a reduction in fish due to overfishing and the risk of losing their boats if they cross international borders. When a young fisherman steps on a boat for the very first time to start his fishing career, he factors in all these risks. Isn't this exactly what an investor does too? We look at the risks that might affect our money and take measures to deal with them.

At 3 a.m., on 26 December 2004, fishermen did exactly what they had been doing every morning – pulling their boats to the sea while praying that the risks they were aware of would play out in their favour. Around the same time, a little off the coast of Indonesia, a massive earthquake struck. It forced waves as tall as 100 feet (a ten-storey building) in all directions. The waves brought down whatever came in their path. This was the tsunami of 2004.

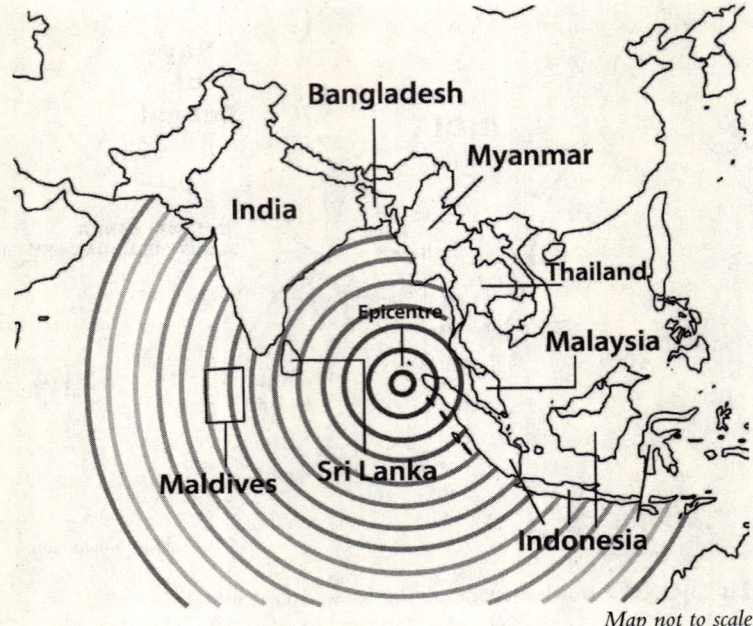

FIGURE 36.3 Areas affected by the tsunami of 2004

Nobody had seen anything like it. It struck every country that was directly in line. Giant waves swept deep into the coastal land, sweeping cars, homes and whatever else came in their path. By the time the total damage was assessed, it was calculated that nearly 2.5 lakh people were dead across different countries. Thousands of fishermen from India and Sri Lanka never came back home. This was a risk nobody prepared for. This was a black swan. Until a certain point in time, the Europeans had only seen swans of white colour. They thought all swans were white. Then, an explorer found black swans in Australia in the 1600s. This was unexpected – something the Europeans thought was not possible.

We prepare for risks we think can affect us. And then we're hit by a risk very few people had thought of but one that affects us greatly – sometimes fatally. Black swan events are incredibly difficult to predict. We're right in preparing for more known risks – they tend to happen more often anyway. But just because you haven't seen something happen doesn't mean it doesn't exist or won't happen. Just like with the white swans, the Europeans and the black swans. Preparing and making yourself strong against possible black swan events is a topic that is extremely controversial. Some believe it is impossible to prepare for black swan events. Some believe we can prepare. Some believe we can be partially prepared. Black swan events as a topic of risk are truly understood by very few.

There is an incredible book on this topic that changed the world of finance (and many other fields) forever – *The Black Swan* by Nassim Taleb. Do you know of a recent black swan that hit us? Financial experts and the media were talking of commodity cycles, GDP growth, stagnation, yield curve inversion and international trade embargoes. Charts and complicated graphs were drawn. Commentaries were made like 'Growth will come back', 'We might see slower growth because of international tensions', 'We're headed for accelerated growth'. And then, something happened that almost nobody was talking about. The black swan emerged. The pandemic.

37

How Does It Scale?

Take two pieces of plastic and tape them together. Effectively, they're one piece now. Now, try pulling them apart. Where did it break? The two pieces would have separated along the length you had put the tape. When you join two pieces, no matter the material (plastic, cloth or metal), the weakest point usually is the point where they were joined.

A certain car manufacturer was struggling with a problem: joining metal pieces. A renowned independent expert had told the media that the car was built using poor practices.[1] As an example, the person spoke of the wheel well. This carmaker had taken nine different pieces of metal and welded them together. Most of its competitors used just one stamped part instead.

The engineers started looking outside the industry for solutions. Body parts of cars are made using a technique called stamping. This is usually achieved by taking a sheet of metal and placing it between two opposite shapes. Then the sheet is pressed, and the metal takes on that shape. (This is how spoons are also made.) A limitation of this process is that complicated designs can't be made. A car's frame is complicated, so carmakers stamp out various parts and then weld them together.

There is another technique that allows complicated parts to be made very fast – die-casting. Many small plastic toys are made using this technique. It uses molten metal instead of sheets. The carmaker enquired whether they could use this method to make the frame of the car. It wasn't possible. There was no die-casting machine in the world that could make something as big as a car's frame. That was a dead end. They placed an order for the world's largest die-casting machine. It was so big that it took twenty trucks to transport it.

The carmaker made the entire car platform (not just the wheel well) using one piece – nobody had done so before. It was lighter and stronger than anything the conventional manufacturing process had produced. The critics stopped criticising.

The die-casting machine's cost was incredibly high. The carmaker will almost certainly recover its investment in this machine as the carmaker is said to be able to make 300,000 (3 lakh) cars in a year. If you're making and selling ten items for ₹50 each (and can't charge higher than this), can you spend ₹4,000 buying tools? If you're making and selling 10,000 items, you can spend ₹4,000 buying tools. That's scale. It simply means, this company, using a factory the size of every other factory and employing the same number of people, can produce a much higher number of cars that are actually better in quality than others while still costing the same. It can also easily increase its production without hiring additional staff. Companies that utilise the power of scaling using a few resources are able to do things that companies with fewer customers just can't.

The internet allows for the craziest examples of scaling. Google Search is used by over 1.5 billion people every day. Google Maps has been downloaded over 5 billion times. Google employs less than 200,000 people. WhatsApp is used by 2 billion people (25 per cent of the world's population). It employs less than 100 engineers. When you are looking at a stock, think about scale. How easy is it for it to scale and reach a larger audience? Can it do that without any significant further costs?

To understand how scale matters, look at the hotel business. When a big 5-star hotel chain wants to expand, they need to buy the properties, hire the staff, set up the supplies and arrange for all other logistics that are part of running a hotel. For ten to twenty new properties with around 400 beds each, they'll take around three to four years at least. For this, they'll have to source funds to pay for the same. If an online hotel or room platform wants to add the same number of rooms and properties to its platform, how much more money does it need to spend? Practically zero. That's how scale works.

38

The Monday Unlike Any Other

MANY OF US REMEMBER the markets crashing in March 2020. On 16 March 2020, the US markets fell by about 13 per cent in a single day.[1] It was triggered by the start of the pandemic that we're still not out of yet. This single-day fall was much bigger than the big shock some investors had seen before that – 2008. On 15 October 2008, the US markets fell about 7.87 per cent in a single day. Neither of these is the biggest single-day fall.

Even when the Great Depression started in 1929, the highest single-day fall experienced was only 12.82 per cent. The largest single-day fall ever experienced was on 19 October 1987: Black Monday. On this day, the markets fell by 22.61 per cent.

- Black Monday (October 1987): −22.61 per cent
- Pandemic (March 2020): −13 per cent
- Start of Great Depression (1929): −12.82 per cent
- Housing crisis (October 2008): −7.87 per cent

What caused this? Let's follow what actually happened that day. It was still night in the US when the markets in Japan opened. As soon as they opened, sharp selling started. As other markets opened, panic began to spread. One by one, markets opened, and seeing what happened in the Japanese markets, the selling started in Hong Kong, Frankfurt, Berlin, London and eventually New York. Just the previous trading day, there had been another fall, but analysts generally expected that to be followed by a rally.

The economic indicators were still nothing to worry about nor was there any political unrest, and there certainly wasn't any virus spreading around. When the markets closed, nobody knew what was happening. It just seemed to have happened. It went down; some people heard it went down, so they started selling. That news spread and even more people started selling.

We know one big reason why this happened: computers! Computers were relatively new to trading back then. Before that, trading was done on the exchange floor by human traders. They would shout, use hand signals and do almost anything to get their trades a match. Then, computers entered the scene. These could place thousands of orders at once. These computers were owned by very large asset managers – insurance companies and other funds. Besides other advantages, computers had been placed to protect investors. What they would do was ensure losses didn't grow too deep. They had been programmed to sell at a certain amount of loss. Since they were not humans, they couldn't factor in any other news. When the losses of their shares reached a certain point, they automatically started selling. That led to more people selling. And that led to other computers selling. Back then, news and information didn't spread as rapidly as it does now.

Today, when there is rapid selling, investors instinctively start looking for a reason behind the fall. Back then, they could not. When there was heavy selling of stocks, they assumed something bad and started selling themselves. Hence some selling somewhere led to more selling somewhere else, led to computers selling, led to more computers selling and more investors selling … that's how you arrive at the worst single-day fall ever – without a valid reason.

Black Monday is why circuit breakers were introduced. Circuit breakers shut down the markets temporarily to stop panic selling. The markets could be halted for a few hours depending on which exchange it is and how much the fall is. They might have been the reason why in the crash of March 2020, the single-day falls weren't bigger than the Black Monday falls. All of this still explains how it played out – not what caused it. The exact true origin of the fall, the reason why the fall truly started, is something nobody knows – even today.

39

Bad Decisions and Good Outcomes

In 2010, it was obvious — smartphones were going to be everywhere. Samsung and Apple were at loggerheads with each other. This was amid fierce competition among phone makers that saw established players fall to their knees (Nokia, BlackBerry). Both Apple and Samsung's phones were spectacular, with top-notch specifications, capabilities, design and materials — everything. That warranted top marketing which in turn decided the prices of the smartphones. At the same time, a brand-new company launched a new phone in China — one that cost one-third of the iPhone. Xiaomi Mi 1. Xiaomi's founder, Lei Jun, was an experienced entrepreneur in China. He had started and invested in multiple companies. He wanted the phone to be top-notch in every possible way. But there was one thing he didn't want to be top-notch — the cost of these phones.

Jun's understanding of the internet, devices, manufacturing and, most importantly, users was unparalleled. Add all of those ingredients and what you get is — Xiaomi Mi 1. An incredibly cheap phone that is almost as capable as three-times-more-expensive phones. Xiaomi had one major cost-saving measure; one that the others thought was unavoidable; one that Xiaomi thought was indeed unnecessary — marketing.

Xiaomi didn't spend any money on marketing. For its first phone, Xiaomi spread the word of its superior specifications and amazingly low price through blogs, online forums and social media. Rapidly, Xiaomi developed a very loud and passionate fanbase. They spread the word further. Within two to three years, Xiaomi became China's biggest smartphone maker.

Xiaomi expanded to other markets in the Southeast like Singapore. After trying those, they finally launched in one of their most significant markets – India. Here too, they adopted the same model – ultra-lightweight. Despite a hard-to-pronounce name, Xiaomi quickly rose and challenged the biggest seller in India – Samsung. By 2015, Indians who'd never used a smartphone in their lives had a Xiaomi in their hands.[1]

A lot was said and written about Xiaomi's ultra-lightweight business model. And then, they hit a wall. Sales were growing, but just not fast enough. The other players were starting to launch phones that matched Xiaomi at their pricing. Xiaomi couldn't reduce their prices further – margins were already too thin for everybody. They did what they themselves thought was unthinkable, and what the others were already doing. Marketing.

In 2015, Xiaomi started with newspaper advertisements. Then came other forms of ads. And then came offline stores. By 2017, Xiaomi had become India's largest smartphone seller. And today, Xiaomi is the world's second-largest smartphone maker, after Samsung. Bigger than Apple. Only behind Samsung. For a long time, Xiaomi, several industry heads and other observers thought Xiaomi's light, no-marketing, no-offline-sales model was the reason behind its success.

They seemed to be right, at least initially. Xiaomi was growing exponentially without marketing. That doesn't mean it was the right decision. Maybe they would have grown even faster with marketing. As investors, whenever we make decisions, it is important to remember something about the nature of decisions.

Imagine you are about to invest in a mutual fund or stock that you have studied and analysed carefully. Right after buying, its price falls. Does that mean your decision was bad? Should you stay away from it and take out your money? Imagine you bought a stock based on a tip from someone else and its price shoots up. Does that mean you made a good decision? Does that mean you should invest more in it? Separate decisions from outcomes. Then judge the quality of the decision.

40

Yes, They Will Fall Someday!

There is never a dull moment in the newsroom. Journalists scout around town, picking up significant stories. Towards the evening, they rush to finish writing their pieces, making sure factual or grammatical errors are removed. Such write-ups are sent to the editor who then, just as fast, edits the piece to be featured in the newspaper the next day. By midnight, the madness ends – for the journalists and the editors.

On the other side, the madness has just begun. The printing press. Rolls of fresh white paper are stacked taller than most people's homes. Gargantuan machines pull in rolls of paper and print whatever the editor has finalised. In a matter of a few hours, lakhs of fresh newspapers get pushed out of the press. The printing press is extremely precise.

One tiny snag anywhere in the chain can halt the entire line. But the newspaper has to be at everyone's doorstep by the morning. Enter the printing press workmen whose ears and eyes learn what others don't even seem to notice. One abnormal click-click sound and the machine grinds to a halt. The workmen's ears pick up these sounds. They know the exact area of the problem (and the solution).

At the other end of the printing press, trucks line up. One chain follows the other and soon your friendly newspaper boy is throwing a rolled-up newspaper at every door – likely while you're still asleep. Recently, a city announced lockdowns around 6 p.m. The journalists began writing their pieces, the printing press, of course, would get to work later that night, and so would others in that line. But everybody already knew.

Many watched a video on their phones, others read an article online and nearly everybody got a WhatsApp forward. Newspapers are being read less. How many twenty-year-olds read the newspaper these days? Everybody is on the internet. Our need for news hasn't changed. But the method we consume that news in has undergone a tectonic shift.

There are independent journalists today who broadcast their own news using social media like YouTube and Twitter. Instead of writing a catchy headline, new-age news bringers go live on Instagram and YouTube. And thus, an entire industry has started dying, while another is taking birth. Thousands of jobs are lost while even more are being created.

All eyeballs, attention, gossip, admiration and criticism used to fall on newspapers. Now they're moving to newer-age media. This is called value migration. And this isn't a rare example. It's happening all the time. It's happening now. Thirty years ago, everybody in the US bought goods from Walmart. Today, Amazon is bigger. People watched television over a cable connection. Netflix and YouTube are changing that.

Which are the fifty biggest companies in India right now? Thirty-seven of the largest companies in India today weren't in the top fifty companies list twenty-five years ago. But of course, this isn't going to be so simple. We know change is inevitable. This begs the question if the companies at the top are going to fall, why not invest in upcoming companies and stay away from the ones that are at their peak?

This happens because there is no known lifetime. We know most humans live for around seventy or eighty years. That's not how companies work. Reliance was one of the biggest companies in India thirty years ago. It still is. Same with banks like SBI and HDFC. Coca-Cola was one of the biggest companies in the world fifty years ago. It still is. There are several others like this.

Yes, they will fall someday. We just don't know when. All companies will eventually die or survive in another version. As investors, we have to keep our eyes open. When the end seems inevitable for our best investments, there will be others that are rising. It is wise to shift when the time is right.

41

Remember This the Next Time You Hear a Dire Prediction

Until a few months ago, there was a fear of hyperinflation. We didn't hear about it so much in our country, but it was a matter of great discussion in America. Hyperinflation refers to an extreme increase in inflation. This is called quantitative easing (QE). A little more casually, QE is also called printing money.

When economies suffer and central banks feel the need to jump-start the economy, they print money. The most recent example of QE is the one done by the US to counter the ill effects of the pandemic-related slowdown. QE has a major feared downside. In short, QE involves the central bank printing money. Print too much money and the economy doesn't gain much since commodities become extremely expensive.

Of course, the central banks don't want to cause this but help the economy get back on track. In America, lumber or wood is of extreme importance – most of their houses are built using lumber. In March 2020, the sawmills that processed lumber faced an important decision. Since the recession of 2008, housing had not picked up and therefore demand for lumber hadn't picked up either.

Staring at another financial crisis, a big chunk of small-company sawmills decided to lay off their staff and shut down or greatly reduce output. A few months into the pandemic, something peculiar happened. The government's printing of money managed to do what it intended to do. People were buying and spending more.

Millions of people working from home resulted in the need to renovate homes, to build another room, to restore parts of the house that weren't holding up well and to buy new houses. The demand for wood started rising. But lumber isn't like water. You can't increase the flow of the tap now and expect more water instantly. Lumber takes months.

Since the mills had cut down production drastically, there was very little wood to go around. And the demand was higher than ever. The prices rose meteorically. When the US started printing money, it attracted a fair number of critics who felt the money printing would lead to hyperinflation. A standard characteristic of hyperinflation is the rising prices of essential commodities.

These critics started pointing towards lumber prices saying that it signalled the start of hyperinflation. They dismissed low production as not the real cause behind the price rise. It used to be in the $500–$600 range. Around May/June 2021, it was around $1,500.

Worry and fear were abound as those predicting hyperinflation cautioned that this price rise would spread to other essential goods; lumber prices were just the start. Sawmills, seeing the skyrocketing prices, started hiring more workers, buying more raw wood and producing more. Months went by, the prices inched up until, finally, the production caught up.

The prices came crashing down. People looking to buy homes or remodel their existing homes rejoiced. The prices reached a range they used to be in. By and large, nobody seemed to notice or care about the people who had predicted the start of hyperinflation with lumber prices. The people who were painting a doomsday scenario have now moved on to other topics.

And yet, the next time they make a new prediction, people will treat their words like they can never be wrong. Remember that the next time you hear a dire prediction. Remember that 'they' is not one person or a group of experts. It is the larger opinion adopted by a vague group of commentators. To understand this better, look up what was said when the yield curve inverted in late 2019.

The yield curve is a plot of interest rates but different maturity dates. When it inverts, many believe a recession is due. It had inverted in 2008. It was touted at the start of the next recession. Nobody said a word when the yield curve went back to normal and there was no recession.

42

Not Keeping All Your Eggs in One Basket Isn't Enough

WHY DO BANKS LET you store money? In addition, they offer you facilities like Automated Teller Machines (ATMs) and net banking. But they don't charge anything. That's because they use your money to make money. Lakhs of people keep their money in the bank. The bank knows that not everybody will come to them asking for all of their money back at once (under normal circumstances). They keep some money aside and use the rest to give out loans – home, car, personal or commercial.

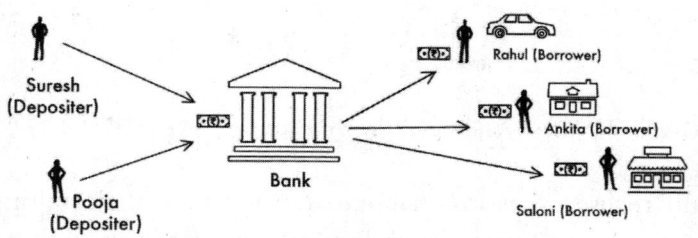

FIGURE 42.1 Ways through which banks make money

They earn interest from these loans. They share some with you in the form of savings interest or fixed deposit (FD) interest and some they keep as their profit. That's how every bank works. Now let's talk about a new concept called securitisation. Instead of keeping the loans with themselves, the bank sells the loan to another institution. Since the bank has sold the loan, it again has money in its hands. It can give out new loans.

The institutions sell these loans to investors who want to earn interest. But here's a problem. How do you know if the loan you're buying is a good one or a bad one? What if the person whose loan you're getting is a person who will default and not pay back? This is called diversification. The institution mixes a bunch of loans together. So instead of one investor buying one loan, a hundred investors buy smaller portions of a hundred loans. Thanks to diversification, the risk is spread out.

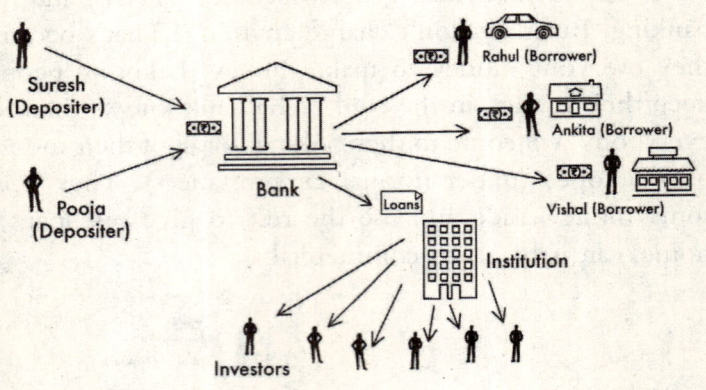

FIGURE 42.2 Banks and securitisation of loans

You realise what just happened? One person defaulting can be disastrous for an individual investor. But one out of a hundred people defaulting is a small dent. In the early 2000s, the banks were doing something similar. They were giving out loans and selling off the loans to institutions who in turn sold them to investors in diversified packages. The institutions had complicated ways of mixing up these loans. One way to understand this would be through the example of a supply shop. A small daily supplies shop owner from New York took a loan and another shop owner took a similar loan, but he was from Chicago.

Considering geographical reasons (storms, weather, other local economic and political conditions), whatever affects Chicago is less likely to affect New York. So, a loan from Chicago and New York mixed together is less risky than two loans from Chicago. This did wonders for the system — at least for a while. This reduction in risk resulted in everyone becoming bolder. Banks started giving out more loans.

Soon they ran out of good people to give loans to, so they started giving out loans to slightly less good people. And then you moved further down to people who were even less likely to pay back. These loans were sold to investors too. A vicious cycle began. More loan-taking pushed home prices up. Higher amounts of loans were given out, and then it imploded.

When enough people weren't able to pay back, people started defaulting. House prices started falling. But diversification would save investors, right? Unfortunately, no. When the house prices started collapsing, it affected the entire country of the US. Diversification didn't really help. From our example earlier, yes, a loan from Chicago mixed with a loan from New York is lower risk, but it isn't exactly a no-risk.

This is what we investors need to make peace with. The same kind of diversification does not always result in lower risk. This isn't about one asset. This is about true diversification. You have one stock. Your friend has ten stocks. Your friend is more diversified and has lower risk. But that doesn't mean if you continue to diversify to a thousand stocks, your risk will go down to zero.

After a certain point, buying more stocks will do nothing to reduce risk. But investing in other assets like bonds, deposits, metals and real estate will reduce your risk, and this holds for every asset you invest in, not just stocks. Think of it like this: you can buy a house near a university to benefit from student rents and diversify by buying a house beside an office to get salaried employee rent. And then another one beside a commercial hub for businessperson rent.

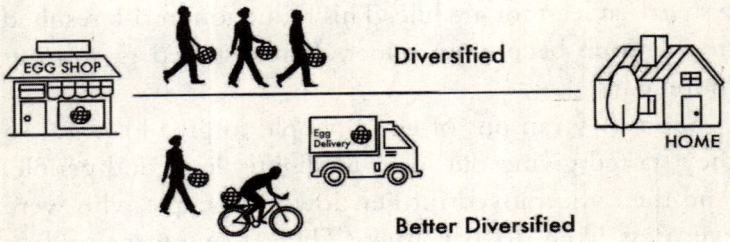

FIGURE 42.3 Investment and diversification

But if the entire city experiences a building-breaking earthquake, you will stop earning rent. Don't keep all your eggs in one basket. Ask different people to carry them in different baskets on different vehicles. Even better.

43

How Much Does a 2BHK in Rural China Affect You?

C HINA HAD A FEW big cities that attracted attention and trade for long. Throughout history, cities have been the birthplace of ideas and all else that happens after a good idea is thought of. To increase economic activity, China has employed one formula excessively: more cities. Shanghai has always been a hub of global trade – around 700 years old. Yet, an internet search gives results that look 20 years old at best.

That peculiarly shaped structure (the first thing you noticed?) is called the Oriental Pearl TV Tower. That and all the others around it didn't exist thirty years ago. This is the futuristic skyline of the Pudong district of Shanghai. It was a muddy and slushy swamp until they built a new city over it in 1993. This build did wonders for their economy. While building the city, thousands were employed. Then, as people moved in, new economies were born.

Shenzhen, a city that didn't exist a little over fifty years ago, borders the much older city of Hong Kong. Now Shenzhen is considered the Silicon Valley of the hardware world. Observing this success, many Chinese construction companies were born who built megacities in no time – everybody knows how fast the Chinese are with infrastructure. Mega skyscrapers were raised in the middle of farms all over the country.

These companies enjoyed the support of the government because these super construction sites employed millions of people and were supposed to give birth to future economies. Around 2015, the Western media started noticing that many of these new cities had nobody living in them – they were ghost cities. Many local governments were able to attract factories and other employers and jump-start their cities' economies. But there were many cities where nobody was living. If nobody was living, how did these builders have the money to continue building city after city?

In China, people noticed the rise of new cities. They invested in real estate. The builders built new buildings, sold them to people who never planned on staying in them, took more loans, built another city, paid back loans using money from the next set of buyers and moved on. This cycle continued till a point. But if nobody is going to live in the cities, the prices of real estate are going to fall.

Soon, these builders will have to pay back all their loans with money not comprised of money made from selling unbuilt houses to future buyers. Real estate forms a ratio of 1:3 of China's GDP. So for a long time, China bailed out these builders. Now, the government is moving its focus towards a sector they believe is more vital for the economy – technology. It is said that the government is clamping down on giant construction companies.

One such company is called Evergrande – a name most of us wouldn't have heard of until a few years ago. This is China's second-largest real estate company. It has taken vast amounts of loans and is now claiming it doesn't have money to pay back. These loans have been taken from all sorts of sources – banks, suppliers, foreign investors, the public and their own workers. It owes over $300 billion. To give you an idea of how much that is, the total market cap of HDFC Bank (total shares multiplied by the price of one share of HDFC Bank) is $135 billion. The GDP of Bangladesh is around $250 billion.

And they can't sell buildings they own because their value has already fallen – nobody wants them. This is being associated with the Lehman Brothers crisis that triggered the 2008 recession. In the middle of last week, this worry caused the markets across the globe to drop. Sensex and Nifty too took a hit. Are we staring at another 2008-like recession? The answer is, as always, very difficult to say. Not every such event turns out to be a recession – most don't.

Brexit was supposed to cause a recession in 2016. So were several others between 2008 and 2020. But they didn't. Experts are divided. Some say it could be a global concern. Some say the fall will be limited to China. Some say it is nothing. For now, it has been dealt with – they paid their immediate debt obligation. But there are more deadlines coming through the rest of this year and beyond. Why does a company defaulting in China affect the rest of us? In short, the same reason a recession in the US affects us.

It might seem odd that 2BHK towers in rural China can affect us, but that is the connected world economy we live in. People new to investing might be surprised at the lack of clarity. They should know that this is how it always is. Prediction is hard and almost nobody gets it right most of the time. Meanwhile, by Friday, concerns about Evergrande seem to have become less of a matter. Most of the global markets recovered. And Sensex went a step ahead – it went up and crossed the 60,000 mark for the first time ever.

44

The Unheard-of Investor Known for Speed

WHAT IS THE BIGGEST amount of money you have gained in the shortest span of time? Bill Hwang was a multibillionaire. How fast did he get rich and how? To get to that, let's understand him a bit better. He was born in South Korea, the son of a pastor. While still a child, he migrated to the US where he attended college and got himself a job in the finance sector. Being immensely talented, he rose through the ranks quickly. Bill worked at Tiger Management – one of the most prestigious hedge funds. When he left Tiger Management, he started Tiger Asia with the full blessings of his bosses.

Tiger Asia did spectacularly well by investing in stocks in China, South Korea and Japan mostly. Using techniques known only to Bill and his team, he'd find stocks that were undervalued and purchase them. In 2012, investigations in the US found Bill guilty of insider trading. Tiger Asia shut down. After dealing with the charges and their repercussions, Bill Hwang left the hedge fund world. He had $200 million with him at this point.

Using this amount, he started Archegos Capital. For someone so high up in the finance world, he has a surprisingly humble lifestyle. He drives a Hyundai SUV (considered cheap in the US), lives in a modest suburban home in New Jersey – similar to most people – and has always been active with his church. Archegos Capital was different from his past work. In the past, Bill had managed other people's money in the form of hedge funds.

Archegos had only Bill's $200 million. It wasn't a hedge fund. It was a family office. What followed is interesting. In just around eight years, Bill grew that $200 million to over $20 billion – 100 times growth in eight years. If you had ₹1 lakh, would you be able to turn it into ₹1 crore in eight years? That's 78 per cent per annum. How did he do it?

The answer is deep fundamental analysis. But Warren Buffett too swears by fundamental analysis. How is it that his wealth hasn't ever grown this fast? Bill Hwang used this one tool that others don't: margin. You have ₹100 to buy stocks. You are sure the stock you want to buy will go up. What do you do? You borrow money and buy the stocks.

Then, once the stocks are up, you sell the stocks, take your profits and repay your loans. This isn't as cumbersome as it sounds. As an investor, you don't actually have to go seek a loan from a bank. It is much more streamlined. Most stock investing platforms offer these loans. They're called margin. In most cases, the amount you can borrow is twice the money you invest. If you have ₹100 to invest, you can borrow another ₹100 to invest.

Margin gives you leverage to turn a smaller amount into a much larger amount. Sounds extremely simple and convenient until the stock you have invested in starts going down. Then your losses are equally big. Loans, margin, leverage – they all cut both ways. They can make you a lot of money. When things go south, they can hurt you like you wouldn't imagine.

Bill Hwang, through financial trickery, had leveraged his stocks five times. For every ₹100 he had, he had borrowed ₹400. Multiple major banks were involved – Goldman Sachs, Morgan Stanley and Credit Suisse. Margin worked brilliantly for Bill Hwang. Until March 2021. Some of his favourite stocks started to go in a direction Bill hadn't planned. In a matter of two days, he lost $20 billion.

Nobody in the history of the world has lost so much money so fast. Absolutely nobody. Imagine being famous for that. The banks that had lent to Bill lost billions as well. Margin can be a great weapon. Margin can be a bad drug too. There's a reason why some very big-name investors do not use margin. Everyone is different. Margin doesn't work for everybody, but it does for some. Tread cautiously.

45

High Returns, but Much Higher Risk

In the 1980s, Alaskan fishermen were in a golden period. Hundreds of ships would go out and spend weeks fishing king crabs, a delicacy that would be exported all over the world. The Alaskan fishermen's lives weren't easy. The sea was extremely rough, and the waves could be much taller than the ships. These were Arctic waters, so the weather was always bone-chilling. Ships would carry metal cages (called pods) weighing hundreds of kilograms. These would be thrown into the water and pulled out using cranes one to two days later.

The weight of the pods would be in excess of 1,000 kilograms with the crabs – as much as a car. The fishermen would then move these pods about aided by a crane on violently rocking ships. The crabs would be kept alive in holding compartments. If one crab died, it would release toxins poisoning the other crabs. So the fishermen would keep a close eye. It was easy for someone's limb to get crushed between two pods. Drowning and hypothermia were the most common ways to die.

When someone passed away, the thought that someday it could be them would send chills down other fishermen's spines. So why were these people risking their lives to bring home this extremely difficult crab? Money. Most people would have already guessed. The crabs sold for prices higher than most fish. The sea had enough crabs for

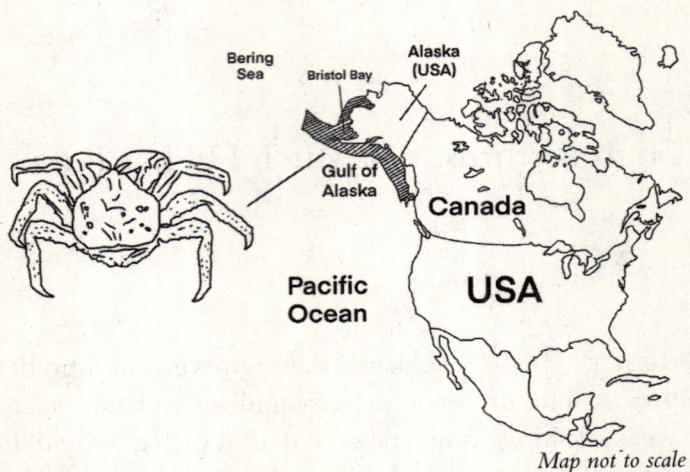

FIGURE 45.1 Areas where king crabs are found in the US

everyone to sell. Hundreds of fishing ship owners would captain their ships into the water with hired deckhands.

These deckhands were no ordinary salaried people. They would get a share of the profits. This made the entire crab fishing experience one where there was no virtual upper limit to the money that could be made. You might notice, so far, everything is written in the past tense. 'It was …', 'It used to be …' and so on. Why did it stop? What happened? What changed? A few things.

First, there was a sudden drop of around 90 per cent in the crab population. Second, fishermen could go out to sea only in one season of about two to three months. Third, restrictions limiting the number of ships were brought in. There were more. These were the main ones. What didn't change was how dangerous this was. These fishing towns and villages that had been crab fishing for years had a culture that revolved around the crabs.

The allure remained. Young deckhands still joined the ships in search of a quick buck. The Bureau of Labor Statistics categorises this job as the most dangerous job in the US. Every year, around 142 people die when considering a total of 100,000 workers – 75 per cent higher than the second most dangerous job. Today, fishing still continues.

After knowing all this, how much is the money? On a good fishing trip, a deckhand can make a few tens of thousands of dollars. That's tens of thousands of dollars in a couple of weeks – something people in those areas make in a year. Are there no other jobs that pay as much for similar levels of education? There are. But in those parts of Alaska, crab fishing is what is viewed as a way to get richer.

In the grand scheme of things, the fishermen are getting richer but not by that much. While what they earn heading out to sea and taking such great risks with their lives is definitely higher than what they would have earned otherwise, what they're ignoring is the risk they're taking. The increase in risk is much higher than the increase in their income. This is a tendency found in investors too.

We look at higher returns and assume the risk has gone up similarly. What if the returns are slightly higher but the risk is significantly higher? High returns, but much higher risk. Now what? Is it still a risk worth taking? Maybe. Maybe not. While making investment decisions, we always measure the returns – low returns, medium returns or high returns.

Very little consideration is given to risk. One of the main reasons behind this is that risk is very difficult to measure. Think of some kinds of higher-return debt funds or Peer-to-Peer (P2P) lending. The returns are higher, but the risk is much higher. What else can you think of? Don't ignore the risk. As the saying goes, it isn't a good idea to pick up pennies in front of a steamroller.

46

More Information Isn't Always Better

The SECOND WORLD WAR ENDED in 1945. The two major forces after the end of the Second World War were the US and the USSR (modern-day Russia). Shaken from the experience of the Second World War, they didn't want a direct conflict. The US was a capitalist country while the USSR was communist. They both wanted to spread their ideologies. Both tried to influence other nations.

The US and USSR competed fiercely in areas of science, industry, space, sports and, of course, military might. Their militaries never clashed. But the countries they supported did fight each other. In effect, the US and Russia were fighting proxy wars. This was the Cold War.

Europe was divided into two parts – the East (USSR supporters) and the West (US supporters) – separated by what was called the Iron Curtain.

By the 1960s, the USSR had set up hundreds of missiles pointing towards Western Europe. In response, the US-supporting countries pointed their missiles towards Eastern Europe. Once either side fired a missile, it would be known to the other side because of missile detection technologies. The fear was, if one side sent missiles at the other, the other side would not wait and would fire missiles back. Both sides would get hit. With the number of bombs each side had, the world would practically end.

More Information Isn't Always Better

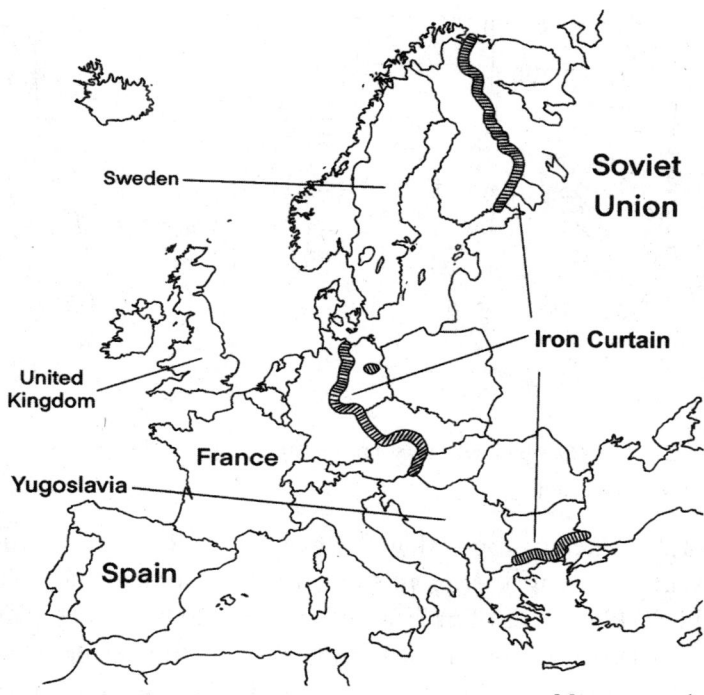

Map not to scale

FIGURE 46.1 Iron Curtain separating Europe into two parts after the Second World War

Both countries had surveillance rooms where trained personnel kept watch for missiles. On 26 September 1983, Stanislav Petrov joined the night shift somewhere in the USSR. Past midnight, the dashboard started flashing – launch detected. Panic spread through the room.

The protocol was to call the seniors and inform them; to tell them that missiles had been fired towards the USSR and to tell them to fire their own missiles towards the US. Stanislav had only thirty minutes to decide. And then, the dashboard indicated a second incoming missile.

There was no time to verify if the information on the dashboard was correct or if it was an error. Then, the dashboard indicated a third incoming missile. Stanislav

FIGURE 46.2 Trained personnel keeping watch for missiles in a surveillance room

and his team knew that once they made a call to their seniors asking to fire missiles, there would be no going back. Hundreds of millions of lives would be lost. A fourth missile was detected. Following that, a fifth missile.

Stanislav and his team discussed all they knew about missiles, detection systems, military strategy and intuition. Stanislav picked up the phone. He informed the person on the other end that there was a malfunction in their system. He did not ask for their missiles to be fired. Much later, it was found he was right. The US hadn't fired any missiles. Their system had malfunctioned.

Stanislav had effectively saved the world. The next day, the stock markets didn't seem affected by this near-apocalypse experience. Newspapers didn't write about it, TV anchors didn't debate it, experts didn't dissect the subject – nothing happened because the night remained a secret for fifteen years.

There are many incidents, both good and bad, that could affect the economy, investments, people's lives, incomes and beyond. But for most of the world, this night holds no significance – because, in the end, nothing happened.

There's a lot of information in this world that points towards something. It may or may not happen. In the modern day and age, we are exposed to a plethora of information. But not all of it is the right kind. What we do with the information and how we react to it is as important as gathering it. That night, Stanislav didn't have time to get his equipment rechecked or to seek a second opinion. Seeing his dashboard indicating five incoming missiles, he concluded that if the US were to attack, they would want to wipe out the USSR completely and would launch many missiles, not just five. He concluded that the missile detection system was at fault.

47

Simple Is Not Easy

Six two-wheeler vehicle riders die every single hour in India. That's more than 50,000 people a year. Moving about is unavoidable. Public transport, though very vast, just isn't enough. Cars are too expensive for the country's price-sensitive population. Hence, two-wheelers. It is quite common to see families of three or four people riding on one two-wheeler vehicle. Needless to say, this is very unsafe. The lawmakers have tried. Certified helmets are mandatory. Only two people are legally allowed. But again, that has not been enough. In that light, another question to be asked is why not make cars cheaper? An effort has been put towards that. Seeing a family of four on a bike getting soaked in the rain, a certain automobile chairman decided to change things. His aim was to make a car that was only slightly more expensive than bikes. A few years later Ratan Tata revealed the Tata Nano to the world.

The Nano, when revealed, wasn't a concept car that would be later made out to be a commercially available product. It was ready. After manufacturing started, the media was given access to the car. Reviews started pouring in from various automobile journalists. Being the cheapest car in the world attracted attention from all over the globe. Some of the biggest names in the auto journalism world had flown to India to experience this wonder – something they wouldn't have done for any other car made by an Indian manufacturer.

FIGURE 47.1 Tata Nano

Journalists soon remarked that the car was incredibly bare-bones. There was no power steering, the seats were simple and bench-like, the engine wasn't powerful, the speedometer was in the centre, there was barely any electronics in it ... it was a very simple car. The remarkable part about the Nano wasn't what it offered. The remarkable part was that it offered a car at a price at which only bikes were available.

Steve Cropley, from *Autocar* (a weekly British automobile magazine), one of the most respected names in the auto world, drove it. What he said sums up everything about the endeavour the Nano was.

> It feels just like a car. The thing you have to keep telling yourself is the price. It really is a terrific achievement. The point that I am trying to make to myself is that nobody

FIGURE 47.2 Tata Ace mini truck

else could do this. The Germans would put in too much stuff ... the Americans would start by pricing it just under the opposition ...[1]

When more people started buying and owning this, they started seeing how Tata had managed to make it so cheap. Instead of four nuts to hold the wheel, it had three. It also had one wiper instead of two. The engine was the smallest in any car in India. It was narrow and small. In hindsight, these decisions sound easy. But they're more difficult to make than deciding what to put in regular cars.

You have to put a small engine in a Nano to keep it cheap — sure. But how tiny? Too small and the car will be useless. Too big and it becomes expensive. Tata re-invented many manufacturing techniques to build the Nano. Even something as industry-standard as the paint was revised. The rest will probably remain industry secrets.

The man responsible for the Nano is one legendary Girish Wagh. Some of his other works include the ever-so-common and equally cheap Tata Ace mini truck. There isn't a corner of India where this vehicle isn't visible. An incredibly common vehicle that everybody seems to find very simple and obvious. Yet, before Tata launched the Ace, nobody had thought of it, let alone make it.

The takeaway is this: simple is not easy. In fact, that which is simple is much harder than many complicated things. In investing, there are several ways to put money to work. Some of the world's wealthiest investors got rich by investing for the long term — a method that is much simpler. You just have to buy the right stocks and wait.

Buying and waiting are simple strategies. Yet in periods when there's a giant downswing, very few can hold on to the stocks they were sure were best for the long term. Not easy. The Tata Nano was a marvel. Yet, due to a few early mechanical issues, bad press and perception, it never really took off. For now, the Nano is dead. Simple is not easy.

48

The Most Quoted Trader of All Time

JESSE LIVERMORE IS REGARDED as one of the greatest traders to have ever lived. More recently, some of his quotes have become popular forwards on social media. He's probably the most quoted trader of all time. Unlike many other investing greats, Jesse isn't alive today. He was active around 100 years ago. He was born in the eastern US state of Massachusetts. At age fourteen, he fled home and got himself a job in Boston as a board boy – someone who posts stock quotes at stock brokerages (no computer screens back then).

Being a fast learner, he caught on quickly. When in that ecosystem, his interest grew towards bucket shops. Bucket shops weren't places to buy or sell stocks; but were places to bet on their movements. At fifteen, he bet on a railroad company. He earned $3.12 in two days (his salary was $6 at that time). By sixteen, he had quit his job and was a full-time trader. Also, most bucket shops had banned him – he was that good.

In about three years, he had been able to generate a return of 1,000 per cent. He tried trading under fake identities but was soon discovered because of his consistent wins. Jesse called himself a speculator, not a trader. He used techniques that are now known as technical analysis. He was basically a trend follower – an extremely good one at that. Jesse stuck to stocks that were moving in a trend – never stuck in a range.

He never invested based on what he felt. He waited for some movement in the markets to confirm what he was feeling before taking action. He always used a stop loss. Sector-leading stocks were his trading picks in a bull market. Weak stocks were his favourite in bear markets. And he never followed too many stocks – that was too much information to process. In 1900, he moved from Boston to New York – a new city, a new start.

In a matter of five days, he converted $10,000 into $50,000. As a trader, he used leverage very liberally. In a recent digest, we've covered how leverage led to the biggest loss in 2021 Young, rich, bold and confident, Jesse was on a roll. In 1901, when he was only twenty-four years old, he anticipated a deep correction and shorted using 400 per cent leverage.

He'd put in most of whatever money he had. There was some delay in updating the board and it affected Jesse's decision-making. He lost everything. He borrowed $2,000 and left the city for another city, St Louis, where nobody knew him. There, he started going to bucket shops again. Hurt from losing it all, Jesse wanted to climb back. He did, very fast. In 1901, he turned $10,000 into $500,000 speculating in another railway stock.

What followed after that was a string of successful bets. He attributed much of his success to sitting and waiting – something other speculators found difficult to do. He grew rich and reached the highest echelons of society. He bought a yacht, a railcar and homes. In 1908, he met Teddy Price who persuaded him to invest in cotton. One of Jesse's beliefs was keeping profit-makers and selling loss-makers.

Oddly enough, while Jesse preached this, he himself struggled to stick to this. All this while, Teddy was slyly selling cotton and Jesse kept buying the loss-making commodity. Jesse lost all he bet. Jesse hated tips. His belief was that a man must trust his judgement. And yet, with cotton, he allowed himself to speculate using Teddy's suggestions. He managed to bounce back – as he always had done.

Every time he hit rock bottom, he spent time understanding what had gone wrong. Those mistakes, he avoided making again. Jesse declared bankruptcy in 1915. Jesse has many feathers in his hat – some he's admired for; some he is infamous for. He was accused of manipulating the market in 1924. He even had the market cornered to the point where the President of the US called him and asked him to stop. In 1929, when the Great Depression set in, he shorted at the right time and made over $100 million.

When the entire country was reeling under an economic crisis, this man made $100 million (equivalent to about $1.5 billion in today's time). In 1934, the Securities and Exchange Commission (SEC) was formed (like we have SEBI). With SEC and its new regulations, Jesse's trading became tough. Then, he made a few wrong bets. When the markets were low, he bet against them, but the markets climbed. When they reached a certain high, he bet for them and the market went down. He lost everything.

In 1934, he filed for bankruptcy again. He managed to settle his tax dues a few years later and started consulting. Jesse once reflected that surviving was the most important rule. He said that it was because he knew he'd make it back that he took such great risks. In 1939, he made another shot at a comeback. In 1940, he wrote a message addressed to his then-wife informing her that he was tired and couldn't fight any longer among other more personal things. After writing that, he shot himself dead.

Jesse Livermore was incredibly smart and wise. But speculation is just such a space and intelligence can only carry a person so far. Eventually, a lot depends on fate. What is necessary is something Jesse preached, but like his other beliefs, failed to follow all the time – surviving is the most important.

49

The Deepest Recession

On 24 October 1929, the US stock markets fell 11 per cent in a single day.[1] Matters eased the next day. But soon, much bigger falls occurred. From the peak reached on 24 October 1929, which came to be known as Black Thursday, the markets eventually went on to fall 90 per cent. It was a recession so deep, nobody in modern history had seen anything like it before – or has ever since. This was worse than the pandemic-induced crisis we saw in 2020; worse than the Great Recession of 2008 and worse than the dot-com bubble of 2000. This was the Great Depression.

It started on Black Thursday. Unlike other recessions we know about that last at best a few quarters, the Great Depression lasted more than ten years. Towards the start of the 1920s, the First World War had just ended, and the supply of money was aplenty. Businesses were expanding, new inventions were changing the way people lived their lives (radio, car and washing machines), and there was a general sense of optimism. Through most of the 1920s, the economic outlook of the US looked very bright. This period came to be known as the Roaring Twenties.

This was also a period when most people had enough money to think about investing. People started investing in the stock markets. As more people piled in, stock prices rose. As stock prices rose, the investors who had invested earlier saw good returns. Those good returns encouraged others to invest further. Soon, the public started borrowing money to invest in stocks. To top that, banks started borrowing money from depositors to invest in stocks!

The valuations reached a point where they seemed unrealistic. At one point, the investors realised the businesses underlying the stocks didn't warrant such high stock prices. Economic activity started suffering a bit and panic spread. This is how Black Thursday happened. Borrowers started defaulting on their loans and because many banks had lent, they started to see defaults.

Over the next two years, several major banks in the US collapsed. Depositors rushed to withdraw their money from the banks, increasing pressure on them. The US government reacted by trying to control the situation. Some protectionist measures were implemented – companies weren't allowed to reduce prices so that they wouldn't reduce salaries. These products and services couldn't compete with cheaper products from abroad. The government tried to restrict some of these cheaper imported items. That made the situation worse as the countries exporting to the US reacted by further hurting economic relations.

Till this point, it might seem like the public's frenzied buying of stocks was the start of all problems. Many argue that wasn't the case. The real problem lay with the Federal Reserve System or the Fed. The Fed was brand new back then and they probably did not have enough experience in controlling the economy. In hindsight, it is believed the Fed committed two major mistakes in handling this situation. Remember, the Fed controls how much money is in circulation in the economy. In India, the Reserve Bank of India (RBI) plays a similar role and has done a great job in handling the recent pandemic-related challenges.

The Fed tries to prevent an economic slowdown or an economic overheat by controlling the supply of money in the economy. The Fed is believed to have allowed too much money into the economy during the Roaring Twenties leading to all the excesses in borrowing. After Black Thursday, in a desperate attempt to control the system, they removed too much money from the system — exactly when more money was needed! This is just one of the reasons for triggering the Great Depression. There is still no broad consensus about all the factors that triggered the Great Depression.

The US government tried to stimulate the economy in various ways but failed to do so effectively. At the peak of the Depression, about 25 per cent of the US population was unemployed. Massive government spending on infrastructure in the mid-1930s helped employ several Americans. Similar measures have since been used by many nations. Even in our nation, government spending on infrastructure employs a large number of people.

Several other measures were also taken to stimulate the economy. Before that, the US government had largely stayed away from the economy. Taxes were raised, business borrowing was supported, the government hired more people to work for them. Finally, towards the 1940s, the economy had recovered enough to be deemed out of the Depression. In 1941, the Second World War started. In the urgencies of war, government spending increased along with cooperation with other countries. Soon, business was booming though the war was another worry for the government.

Many believe the Second World War ended the Depression. This isn't true though. It did help in economic growth and recovery, but a lot of the recovery had started taking place even before the war. The Depression was such a period, it impacted an entire generation and changed the way they functioned. Even to this day, it is common to see senior citizens who lived through the Depression era lead extremely frugal lifestyles.

What followed was an era of excess and economic growth. The US, nor the world, has seen a crisis as bad as the Great Depression. The pandemic in 2020, many feared, would have resulted in something similar. But thankfully, it seems that isn't happening. The point of this is to tell you what the Great Depression was. It isn't connected to the situation today and we're not trying to indicate anything about the present economic conditions.

50

What Happened in 1992?

ABOUT THIRTY YEARS AGO, an incident took place in India that changed the way the Indian stock markets worked: Harshad Mehta. While most Indian investors know about this event, they don't quite understand how it happened and what changes it caused. As a young man, Harshad wasn't involved in the stock markets. He started his career working multiple jobs in Mumbai before finding his way into the New India Assurance Company as a salesman. He was introduced to the markets when he joined a brokerage firm in the early 1980s. Over the next ten years, he rose through the ranks. He eventually quit his job and started his own brokerage firm.

FIGURE 50.1 Stockbroker Harshad Mehta

In the markets, price is driven by demand. A stock's price shoots up when more people want it. The opposite also happens. This is basically the reason why any stock goes up or down. Individual investors alone can't really affect the price of a stock. But a large number of individual investors can affect the price of a stock – and they do. And, if one or a small number of investors have a lot of money to buy or sell stocks, they can affect the price too. How much is 'a lot of money'? That varies from stock to stock.

Back in Harshad's days, there was a rule for banks. They had to hold a certain percentage of their total assets in government securities. The government needs money to build infrastructure and carry out other tasks. So often, they borrow money from banks while promising a certain interest rate – just like any other loan. These are called government securities. Due to the banks' operations, some found it difficult to maintain their allocation in these government securities, so they would pay money to other larger banks and borrow the government securities from them. They would also pay interest for this. Now, we understand that banks borrow these government securities from each other in exchange for money. To do this, banks made use of brokers – stockbrokers. Brokers had excellent networks, and they could connect banks in need of government securities to banks that would lend in exchange for some money.

Harshad Mehta had a vast network. He was the perfect man for the job. He started connecting these banks to each other. Think again: banks need certain levels of government securities, so they exchange securities for money. These deals are brokered by stockbrokers. Harshad Mehta commanded an incredible level of trust in the system. The banks would write money to Harshad Mehta. To both sides, he would promise to find a deal in a few days. In those few days, he'd take that money and buy stocks. This was so much money that it would cause the stock price to rise. Seeing the price climb, other investors would flood money into buying the stock. Then, at a higher price level, market participants would sell off their shares and exit – making money in the process.

This worked well for some time. He had a large network of banks to work with so he would take money from one bank, put it in the stock market, take more money from another bank and return some of the earlier banks' funds. The markets kept climbing and Harshad managed to pay everyone back on time. Then, the markets got a hint about this. Sucheta Dalal, a journalist, unravelled the scheme and wrote a report on it on 23 April 1992. The markets started crashing. The stocks Harshad had invested humongous amounts of banks' money in started to crumble. He couldn't return the money. The Central Bureau of Investigation (CBI) started investigating the matter and he was put behind bars. He remained in jail for years and in 2001, he died of a heart attack.

This event led to many monumental changes in the system. The Securities and Exchange Board of India (SEBI)widened its jurisdiction by a big margin to include Foreign Institutional Investors (FIIs), venture capital, credit rating agencies and more. Stock investors now need to maintain a minimum balance to buy stocks – this was not required back in the day. The entire transaction process is online now, making it more transparent. And finally, one of the biggest changes came in the settlement period. Once a stock buy–sell deal takes place between two parties, the trade is locked but the actual transfer of the stock happens much later. This is called the settlement period. In Harshad's time, it was transaction date plus fifteen days, or T+15. The brokerage firm had to pay the money fifteen days after a transaction was placed through them. This gave a lot of leeway to brokers. Back then, this scheme allowed various brokers to do other things with the money that was with them. Today, this is much tighter at T+2 days. In just two days, it becomes incredibly hard for such an activity to take place. T+2 days is the standard all over the world including the biggest stock market in the world – the US. SEBI has mandated an even tighter one-day settlement cycle from February 2022: T+1.

51

Journey from Start to IPO and Beyond

THE MARKET IS FILLED with IPOs this year (2021). For the Indian investor, there is something relatively new: internet company IPOs. Internet companies surprised investors when they were new back in 2000 in the US. Something similar is happening in India now. How do these internet companies reach the IPO stage and what happens after?

Until the internet became commercialised and revolutionised the way the world worked, companies took a long time to become big. Building something big just takes time. Take a supermarket chain or a telecom company. You can't just launch a new product and spread it across the country. It takes time to gradually set up offices and warehouses, lay the groundwork, hire thousands of people and organise supply chains. Internet companies work much faster. A handful of workers can make something on their laptops and launch it to the entire globe in a matter of weeks. Those who saw the potential in internet companies early invested and moved fast. Then others realised the opportunity and tried to cash in.

Today, the journey of internet companies works very differently – it is extremely organised and smooth compared to other sectors. Travis Kalanick felt the luxury limousine market in the US was very unorganised. He decided to build a company in this space – an internet company. Now, when you build a company, you need money. You can either get that from your own pocket, borrow from friends and family, or borrow from a bank. There's one more way. You can sell shares of your company. You can't sell these shares on the stock markets or exchanges – that's not allowed because you barely have a business at this point. But outside the stock markets however you can sell shares of the company to willing buyers. Individuals who invest in such companies are called angel investors. Institutions that invest in such companies are called venture capitalists. Angels and venture capitalists invest in very early-stage startups after seeing the potential in them – even when there's almost nothing in the business to show for it.

It's not like angel and venture investors aren't governed. Regulatory bodies have regulations for them too – although they're a bit more relaxed than the rules for retail investors. Angel and venture investing are incredibly risky and at the same time require large investment amounts. In exchange for their investment, angel and venture investors get some percentage of the company, which is not fixed. It is negotiated in every deal. Back to Travis and his limousine company.

In August 2009, Travis launched UberCab – an application through which you could hail luxury limousines. Among the rich and technologically savvy of California, it was an instant hit. In October 2010, the company raised more money: $1.25 million. They also renamed themselves from UberCab to just Uber. Again, some portion of the company was given to investors in return for money. This means, every time a company raises money, the ownership percentage of the existing shareowners – company founders like Travis and other investors who joined earlier – reduces. So, every time he raises money, he's reducing his ownership of the company.

Why does the founder agree to reduce their ownership? At this stage, they aren't making any profits. And they need money to survive and grow.

With this fresh money, Uber starts expanding to other cities in the US. Somewhere along this journey, it moves beyond the luxury limousine market and enters the mainstream cab business. It is immediately met with resistance from local taxi unions. But the company manages to operate and expand. It starts spending money on operations, new offices and employees, advertisements, driver incentives and passenger discounts. The expansion needs more money. They go back to raise money again. A bunch of venture investors invest $11 million. Why? Because they see growth. They see that the company is burning money and not making a profit but once it is done expanding, there will hardly be any business like this one – so it can be very profitable.

New challenges are born for the company. It soldiers on. It expands more, it hires more people, it opens even more offices and it reaches even more cities. Investors see promise and more money is invested by other investors. Uber manages to change the way people move around in cities across the world. Nearly all major cities in India have Uber, as do many other Asian cities and almost all American and European cities.

Uber also sees some scandals. Senior folk of the company are accused of various wrongdoings. Drivers revolt against reductions in incentives. Passenger discounts are reduced so that the company can cut its losses. All of these invite criticism and protests. But the company is expanding at breakneck speed which means it'll have a reach and network unlike any other, and it could potentially have unbelievable profits someday. Investors put more money into Uber. At each investment round, the ownership percentage of the founders (Travis and others) decreases.

One controversy leads to another, and Travis Kalanick is asked to leave the company. A new CEO is appointed and tasked with continuing the journey of the company.

This is the point where things get a bit new for Indian investors. Then, the company decides to go for an IPO – while still being a loss-making company. The IPO went live in 2019. Why would investors want to own a loss-making company's shares? For the same reason the angel and venture investors kept investing – they think the future of the company has great profits. This journey of raising money from investors multiple times and then eventually going for an IPO is one that most internet companies have undertaken – Google, Facebook, Amazon, Airbnb, Paytm and Zomato. Building an internet company requires massive amounts of money that is almost impossible to borrow from other sources. Raising funds from angel and venture investors is the industry-standard practice.

In its journey so far, Uber has raised a total of over $20 billion. Every single year since then, the company hasn't made profits – until November 2021 when it finally showed some profits. Does that mean it'll continue to show profits from now on? Time will tell. Amazon took several years to show a profit after its IPO. At the time of its IPO, it was priced at around $1.7. Today its stock price is around $3,600. Facebook was profitable more or less from the year of its IPO. At the time of its IPO, it was priced at $42. Today, it is at $345. There are IPOs like TheGlobe.com and Pets.com. These are massive internet companies that reached the IPO stage while being at a loss and then continued to remain profitless till they died.

Why did we cover Uber and not Amazon, Facebook or Google's story? Because those are already successful. Uber is where many Indian internet companies heading for IPOs are – loss-making but with great reach and network potential. Each internet technology company is different. What will happen to Uber from here? That's for each investor to decide and for time to tell. The same goes for all other companies they might be thinking of investing in.

52

The Advice That Didn't Work in Japan

INVEST FOR THE LONG term. This is a line you hear incredibly often – especially with stocks and mutual funds. Why is this true? Or is this even true? For large economies, this has been true. The US is the biggest example of this. And there are several others. At this point, the one country many look at with curious eyes is Japan. Japan has been one of the largest economies in the world for a while now and despite that, it is the one glaring example of a stagnated economy.

To understand Japan's economy, we need to go back to the Second World War. The US dropped two nuclear bombs on Japan in 1945 – an event that changed the world. In the years following this event, Japan started building everything. It received aid from the US which triggered its industrial revolution. Some of the most popular high-technology brands you've heard of came out of Japan in that era – Sony, Panasonic, Toyota, Honda and Yamaha.

In the 1960s, Japan's GDP was growing at a rate of 10 per cent per annum which was unheard of.[1] Japan became synonymous with incredible technology which helped the economy become more efficient and grow even faster. The growth lasted for decades. At its peak, Japan was flying so high – its real estate market climbed to astronomical values. The Imperial Palace in Tokyo occupied an area of more than 4 square kilometres – its real estate value was more expensive than the real estate value of the entire state of California (more than 4 lakh square kilometres).

Japan was an exporting powerhouse, and its biggest customer was the US. Customers in the US were buying Japanese electronics, cars and other products. Then, in a five-year period during the 1980s, the US dollar versus Japanese yen exchange rate suffered. Exporting items from Japan to the US became tougher. This meant that the Japanese economy would suffer since so much of it depended on exporting to the US. They tried to change the flow of demand and instead of relying on US exports to support their economy, they looked inwards.

In the decades since this massive industrial revolution started, Japan's population observed an upgrade in lifestyle like no other. This middle-class population could easily spend money buying many goods that were now deemed essential – washing machines, TVs and cars. To encourage this behaviour, Japan lowered interest rates. Central banks all over the world use interest rates as a tool to control the economy. What happens when you reduce interest rates? People borrow more and spend more. This result was achieved. People started buying far more goods and services. They also started investing in real estate and stocks. When excess cash flows into the markets, the markets rise, that is exactly what happened.

At its peak in 1990, the Nikkei reached around 38,000 points (their version of the Nifty 50). At that level, everybody knew the markets were extremely overvalued. A gradual cool-down of the economy was attempted. But a gradual cool-down it was not. In a two-year period, the markets fell by over 60 per cent. So far, everything seems familiar to whatever we've heard about past market bubbles. Here's where it gets different.

When investors ask experts about when to invest and when not to, the usual answer is 'Just invest for the long term.'

The Advice That Didn't Work in Japan

Because in the longer run, the growth is such, the downturn or bubble and recovery doesn't even matter. This has been true for all major economies: the US, India and the European Union (EU). In Japan, the markets reached 38,000 in 1990 and fell. Even to this day, thirty years later, they haven't recovered. It's around 30,000 right now and there are many theories as to why this happened.

Japan has a population problem: people live long lives and aren't having enough kids. So, their population is increasingly older and there just aren't enough people to work while there are too many who need support. This is often mentioned as the reason behind their economy not recovering. Additionally, the Japanese markets have given good returns over a fifty-year period. The rise in 1990 was abnormally high so that couldn't have been beaten so fast. Some say Japan advanced so fast, it reached the best possible state very fast, leaving very little room for further growth.

Every financial expert dreads having someone ask them about the Japanese economy. The truth is, we know what happened. But nobody can truly say why it happened. This is a humble reminder, no matter who you ask, nobody has all the answers. If you leave Japan aside, there is no modern major economy where investing for the long term hasn't worked. Even in Japan, if you hadn't invested all your money between 1986 and 1993, you would still be sitting on returns higher than what you would get by investing in bank deposits in Japan.

53

Rules That Stopped Making Sense

When you have to tell someone they have a call, how do you signal? This hand gesture describes it perfectly. It looks very appropriate. The thumb is for the earpiece and the little finger is the mic.

FIGURE 53.1 Hand gesture to signal a call. The thumb acts as an earpiece and the finger acts as the mic

But most of us barely use landline phones these days. Isn't this hand gesture outdated? Ask someone young in your house, someone born in the 2000s, to make a hand gesture using a phone. Chances are the hand gesture they use will look like this: the entire palm, with fingers held closely, is held close to the ear to depict a smartphone.

Isn't this more appropriate for the smartphones we all use? Why is it that we're still using an outdated gesture? We're just habituated to it. The sneaky thing about habits and rules is that once we're sure they work for us, we put them on autopilot – we never think about them.

Warren Buffett has some rules he follows. A stock's price is centred on the business a company does. This is where valuation comes into the picture. This is a vast field you can spend weeks learning but in short, it's a measure of a stock's price being fair (or not fair). The price-to-earnings (PE) ratio is one of the most popular metrics to measure valuation, though it isn't the only one. So, if too many people buy a stock, its price rises. The higher its price rises, the higher its valuation is, unless its earnings also rise.

There's a certain style of investing – value investing – that pays great attention to the valuation of a stock. The idea is to buy stocks that are undervalued and sell stocks that become overvalued. Of course, it isn't that easy. There is no 'right' valuation. There is no clear definition of overvalued and undervalued. It's subjective. Each investor's definition of overvalued and undervalued varies.

Warren Buffett is famous for his comments on valuation and is known for sitting on vast amounts of cash and not investing because he felt the markets were overvalued. Warren Buffett, possibly the greatest investor of our time, has this rule: never invest in overvalued stocks. He also has another rule: stay within your circle of competence. This means Warren doesn't invest in stocks from every industry. He sticks to the sectors he deeply understands.

In the late 1990s and early 2000s, a new kind of stock came to rise: internet technology stocks. Warren cautioned about the exceedingly high valuations of technology stocks. He stayed away from them. Turns out he was right. The dot-com bubble popped and within a few days, many internet companies' share prices crashed. Many of those companies shut down forever. The investment portfolios of many investors took giant hits. Not Warren's. Having been proven right, Warren stayed away from internet stocks after the dot-com bubble too.

Warren Buffett deeply admired Jeff Bezos for creating and running Amazon. He was wildly optimistic about the company. But the Amazon stock price was always in a range that Warren deemed overvalued, so he never invested. In 2008, Warren's cautious approach was validated again when the Great Recession hit. Even after the dot-com bubble of 2000, the internet technology stocks managed to reach a level where Warren would simply not look at them. It still seemed like a bubble to him.

In the 2010s, seeing the internet technology stocks rise meteorically, Warren realised that technology stocks worked differently, and he was very open about his inability to understand them. That would have been fine – he could have just invested in stocks of sectors he thought he was an expert in. But the returns were too high to ignore. In 2016, after shying away from technology stocks for nearly all his life, he started buying Apple stocks. He kept on buying stocks of Apple – a sector he said he would stay away from. Today, over 40 per cent of his total investments are in Apple.[1]

Buffett has made over $100 billion from investing in Apple in the last five years. There is no other stock in this investor's portfolio with more money in it. He owns about 5 per cent of Apple, making him the biggest investor in the company. He also owns chunks of Amazon. One of his most recent big technological investments is a company that opened its IPOs — Snowflake. Warren Buffett has broken his own rules. Times change, people evolve, conditions convert and rules die. Rules save time and effort, but every now and then, it makes sense to ask: why does this rule exist?

54

The J-Curve of Internet Companies

Facebook was born in Mark Zuckerberg's hostel room. When most people picture this, they imagine a brand-new company that was a runaway hit from day one. However, most successful tech startups begin at a point of uncertainty and go through a journey that involves steps that are anything but certain. The concept of this journey is explained very well by the American entrepreneur Howard Love. He calls it the startup J-curve. He divides this journey into six parts.

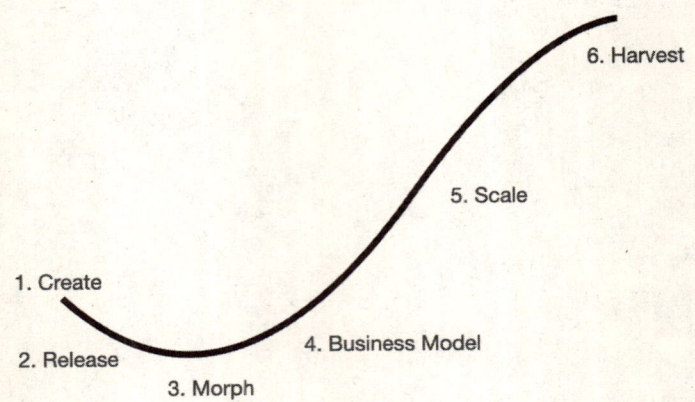

FIGURE 54.1 Howard Love's startup J-curve

The first part is creation. At this stage, the company is nothing but a dream. The founders have an idea, they set up a team (usually very small and made up of only the co-founders) and arrange for money. Where does the money come from? Many times, founders use their own money. There are also investors who invest in such companies for a sizeable stake. These investors are usually venture capitalists. They invest in startups that are loss-making but have the potential to generate massive amounts in the future. This is an exciting stage because, at this point, everything seems possible. Whatever the idea is, it does not yet exist as a product or service. It's a dream in the heads of the founders. However, many startups don't get any money from investors at this stage.

The second part is release. This is where many startups release an initial version of their idea to the world – to whomever they want to target. A very large number of startups get funded at this stage. Think of some very big names like Airbnb, WhatsApp, Facebook – they all had their release first and then came the funding. The release doesn't mean their product was a grand success upon launch. Often the case is the opposite. But at this stage, you can get a glimpse of what the team is capable of and what it might be able to do. This is what baffles a lot of people who aren't in this industry. Why invest in something that doesn't work yet? Being early to a possibly successful technology business has massive benefits, and these investors are willing to take giant bets to gain those benefits.

The third part is morph. For many startups, things can look a bit dark at this stage. After their idea is made into a product and released, the team learns about how it actually fares in the real world. Almost always, their first version never works. It requires changes. If they're lucky, the changes might be small. But most have to go through large changes. Many startups change so drastically at this stage that it is unbelievable when you compare their final version to their initial version. Facebook started off as a social network only for college students. Myntra, the e-commerce fashion company, started off as a custom

T-shirt printing company. Zomato started off as a restaurant menu and contact book. They changed in between. Some went through changes multiple times before arriving at their final version.

The fourth part is the business model. Now, even if a product works, how will the company make money? To many who aren't exposed to this industry, the idea that a company was started without a business model in mind is unfathomable. But this is how things work in the modern technology domain – you get the audience's attention first. Everything else can be worked out later.

Let's go back to Facebook. How does it make money? It was free till this stage. It still is. But then it wasn't making money, and through various experiments and tests, they figured the best way to make money was to have ads on their platform.

The fifth part is scale. This is where the magic truly starts. If the company has played its cards right, things should start working now. This is where scale comes in – something that was alien to most companies in the pre-internet era. When any other business is started, the founder will have to hire some people. Similarly, when any other business wants to expand, the company will have to hire a lot more people.

A tech startup might not have to hire anyone or hire only a few people. The speed and size of a tech company's spread usually vary. Imagine McDonald's. To expand all over the world, it would take so much effort – find real estate, find suppliers, hire employees, etc. Facebook had the same number of people working at their offices when they had 1,000 users and 10,000 users. And only a few more were hired when they went on to millions of users. This is exactly why tech companies are so different. This is why investors are willing to invest millions of dollars in loss-making startups. It is to help them build their product without worrying about paying salaries.

From the outside, it looks strange. There's a company that doesn't have a business model, doesn't even have a fully functional product, but it requires money every day. This view makes sense, and this stage is also where many companies die because whatever they built didn't work. But the few companies that make it from here make it big, with astronomical returns. For venture capitalists who invest in several money-eating startups, usually, a small number of successful investments is enough to cover their investments in failed startups while still making astronomical returns.

The sixth part is harvest. The company has become what many people think of as a company at this stage. It is making money; it has established patterns and methods. This is the stage where companies open their IPO. That brings us to the end of the J-curve. Except things are a lot more complicated than this (of course). A company needs money to run. Whatever money it has gained from investors, eventually, runs out so it has to either make profits or raise more funds. An IPO is a way to raise some money too. Many companies move the IPO stage ahead in the J-curve and don't necessarily wait till the sixth stage. When Amazon IPO'd, it was at this stage; so did Uber and Zomato.

Remember these three things about the startup J-curve:
- Most companies go down before they go up.
- Most companies are trying to raise money through the parts of the J-curve.
- Companies can fail or succeed at any point in the J-curve.

55

Is It a Pond or Is It an Ocean?

A PAIR OF SHOES WORTH ₹2 lakh is not exactly a necessity. By any measure, it won't make rational sense to buy shoes that cost that much. A 150-year-old brand named John Lobb has shoes that usually start at this price. Much like several legacy brands that are older than a century, John Lobb is actually the name of the founder. 'Shoes that last a lifetime' is their call to fame. But anyone with a little bit of awareness would be quick to point out that nobody buying John Lobb shoes cares as much about them lasting a lifetime. John Lobb's shoes are a status symbol.

John Lobb, as a young person, learned to make shoes as an apprentice. Gradually, as he got better, he opened his own practice and started making shoes. Unlike how shoes are made now, John Lobb would tailor-make each pair with exemplary fit. Even today, the process hasn't changed much. Once you have an appointment, the measurements of your feet are taken. For this, you'll have to visit their London location. If you're important enough – like many of John Lobb's customers are – someone will come to you (wherever you are). Chances are that the person measuring your feet would be someone whose last name is Lobb – the setup is still run by John Lobb's descendants.

FIGURE 55.1 An apprentice learning shoemaking

Measurement is taken and special attention is given to the joints in your feet, the arch, the asymmetry of the two feet, the shape of the back of the feet and other details we wouldn't know of. Then, the measurements are used to make lasts, which are essentially wooden models of your feet. Your leather shoes will be made around these wooden lasts that are an extremely close replication of your feet. It takes a few months for someone at John Lobb to make your shoes by hand. You have several options to choose from – the style of heel, leather, colour, closure and whatnot. The lasts are stored in case you want another pair at a later point in time.

Despite such elaborate procedures, the company faced stiff competition from modern-day shoemakers. In the 1980s, they also started offering factory-made shoes. Those shoes possess many of the traits of their handmade shoes. Despite that, chances are most people you know have never heard of this brand. But they would have heard of Nike. Nike has always gotten its shoes made in factories. There are shoes meant specifically for different occasions like casual wear, running, sports. But they're rarely designed for any specific pair of feet.

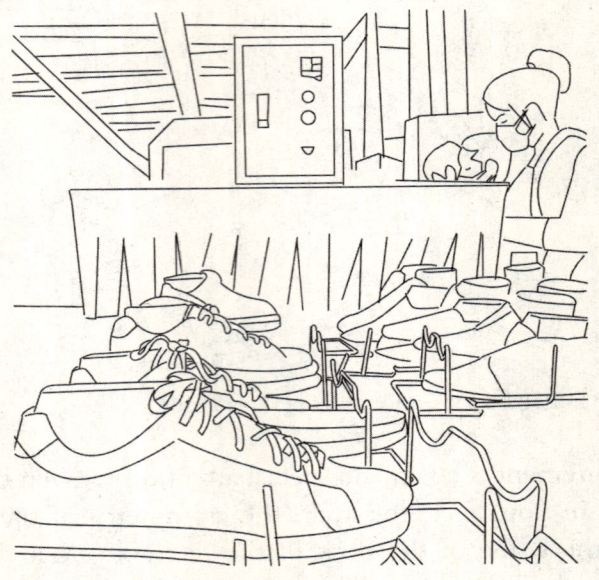

FIGURE 55.2 Factory-made John Lobb shoes

The shoes are just cheap enough that the middle class can afford them making them a premium wear option for the masses. The number of rich people who can buy John Lobb is very small. The number of middle-class people who can buy Nike is extremely large. Compared side by side, a John Lobb customer is more likely to rain praise on John Lobb for the immaculate fit and finish, excellent quality and eclectic design. Who makes more money per shoe? John Lobb does. Who makes more shoes? Nike does. Who does? Nike.

Charlie Munger famously said, 'The first rule of fishing is: fish where the fish are.'[1] No matter how good you're at something, the results will still depend on the size of the opportunity. If you go catching fish in a pond with just ten fish, the maximum number of fish you can catch is ten. Never more than that. Alternately, if there's a pond with millions of fish, even a beginner might catch 100 fish. This isn't to say John Lobb is doing it wrong. They're probably doing what they want to. It's just to show that the size of the opportunity matters. If an investment's best-case growth is small, no matter how well you research, your investment isn't going to go that far. Always invest where the possible growth is very to extremely high.

56

All That 2021 Was

Today is the last sunday of 2021. Last year, on the last Sunday of 2020, in the 'Groww Digest', we'd covered the biggest events of 2020. The year 2020, beyond belief for most of us, brought many learnings. While 2021 isn't very different, the second half of the year has been a little less eventful (thankfully so). Here's Groww Flashback 2021:

- 1 January 2021: Things are starting to look up. The US has started vaccination, and we hear India too will start soon. The number of new cases is falling sharply, and the markets have touched all-time highs (Sensex is around 47,000).
- 12 January: Tesla sets up office in India – something Indian fans were eagerly looking forward to.
- 16 January: Vaccinations start in India with frontline workers being the first to be eligible.
- 25 January: News of new variants discovered in South Africa and Brazil spreads. This is the first time newer variants of the virus are being discussed and being looked upon as threats.[1]
- 27 January: ByteDance (parent company of TikTok) shuts its India office after the application was banned in 2020.
- 28 January: The GameStop short squeeze takes place. Hedge funds are caught off guard.

- 1 February: Budget is presented in the Parliament. It is generally well-received. Markets close over 4.7 per cent up.
- 7 February: New case numbers bottom out at around 8,500 cases. From this point on, the numbers climb steadily for the next few months.
- 24 February: An infrastructure-related glitch leads to a four-hour halt in trading on NSE. The exchange later identifies the cause and rectifies it.
- 26 February: Markets fall almost 4 per cent in a single day as fears of the new variant are a cause of concern for everyone. In the next few weeks, the markets dipped sharply for a few more days due to the same delta variant.
- 1 March: Vaccination starts for senior citizens and for those above forty-five years of age with co-morbidities.
- 8 March: Maharashtra and Karnataka reduce stamp duty charges to encourage real estate purchases, and a critical SMS delivery failure takes place in the country which results in many important transactional SMS like OTPs not reaching users.
- 22 March: The government increases the gap between two doses of Covishield from four weeks to eight weeks.
- 25 March: A sharp increase in the number of cases reported is observed. It is almost clear at this point that a second wave is on its way in the country.
- 29 March: The ship blocking the Suez Canal is finally freed allowing cargo ship movement to restart.
- 1 April: Vaccination for everyone above the age of forty-five years starts.
- 5 April: The single-day number of cases reported is 1.03 lakh – this is higher than the highest one-day cases reported during the first wave.

- 15 April: Citigroup announces it will shut its banking operations in India. As a clear second wave occurs in India, the markets remain more or less stable with Sensex hovering a little below the 50,000 mark – no major fall is observed despite the second wave. Unlike the first wave, flights remain operational too.
- 29 April: SEBI announces a new rule which requires fund managers to receive 20 per cent of their pay in the form of units in mutual funds they manage.
- 1 May: Vaccination for all above the age of eighteen opens up. In the middle of the second wave, there is a severe shortage of vaccines.
- 6 May: Almost 4.14 lakh cases are reported in a single day. This is the highest single-day case number reported ever. Numbers start falling soon after this.
- 13 May: The dose gap for Covishield is increased from eight weeks to twelve to sixteen weeks.
- 1 June: The MET announces that 2021 will see above-average rainfall in the monsoons.
- 10 June: Around 1 lakh cases are reported in a day – only about a month after 4 lakh cases were reported.
- 22 June: The National Company Law Tribunal (NCLT) approves the Jet Airways resolution plan.
- 1 July: Covishield gets a green pass – travel to Europe becomes possible for Indians.
- 7 July: The central government reshuffles the cabinet. Forty-three new ministers take the oath.
- 13 July: The highest ever export from India in a month is reported – $35.43 billion in July
- 23 July: Zomato IPO gets listed. This is a monuments day as a homegrown tech startup enters the Indian stock markets.
- 29 July: Fears about a third wave start doing the rounds as nearly 50 per cent of all new cases are reported from Kerala.

- 5 August: The government announces the nullification of retrospective taxes[1] – an issue that had deeply affected Vodafone and Cairn. In the meantime, demand for cars and bikes had climbed back up sharply but companies were struggling to meet the demands. The issue of chip shortages that started last year was still not resolved. As of writing this at the end of 2021, it is still unresolved with orders piling up at carmakers.
- 9 September: Ford India announces a major restructuring of its India operations which involves stopping car production in the country. Ford says it would continue to operate as a premium vehicle company in India.
- 13 September: Jet Airways announces its plan to restart its operations in the first half of 2022.
- 5 October: Moody's upgrades India's rating to 'stable'.[2]
- 6 October: The government allows 100 per cent foreign direct investment in the telecom sector via the automatic route.
- 8 October: Tata wins the bid for Air India.
- 11 October: Akasa Air gets approval to start operations.
- 21 October: India announces administering a total of 1 billion vaccine doses.
- 3 November: COVAXIN, the only widely administered vaccine developed in India gets approval from WHO.
- 15 November: The first-ever parliamentary-level meeting on cryptocurrencies takes place. For a few years now, the government's stand on crypto has been unclear. Even as of writing this, it remains unclear though there appears to be a reasonable softening in its stand against crypto.
- 10 November: Nykaa lists on the Indian exchanges. Its IPO was oversubscribed eighty-two times.
- 18 November: Paytm lists on the Indian exchanges. It is the biggest IPO ever. Tech IPOs are a relatively

new concept in India. With these few IPOs, Indian investors are learning about and warming up to the tech start-up scene brewing in India.
- 29 November: A new variant called Omicron is discovered and starts spreading alarm as the number of mutations is incredibly high. Markets the world over tank in fear. At the same time, early data about the relatively less severe nature of this new variant also start surfacing.
- 9 December: Inflows into equity mutual funds start reaching higher levels as more investors start feeling confident about investing.
- 25 December: The prime minister announces a booster dose for frontline workers and children above fifteen years of age.

Sensex started the year at around 48,000. Right now, it is around 57,000 – up by around 20 per cent. We don't know what the future holds for us. Nobody knows. But looking at how the past unfolded gives us ideas that help us prepare for the future. It also gives us hope – the markets have proven to be far more resilient than many of us thought. On the upside, the markets do make you smile when you least expect them to.

57

Why Does Gold Have Value?

There is about 2 lakh tonnes of gold on the planet in use today. That isn't a lot in comparison to other metals. Around 50 per cent of that is in the form of jewellery, 35 per cent is in the form of investments (gold bars, biscuits and coins) and the remaining 15 per cent is in industrially produced products.

Why is gold valued so much? Gold has some practical uses: it is used in the circuits of electronic devices, medicines and a few other products. That's where 15 per cent of all the mined gold is. But these uses have come only in the last thirty to fifty years. Gold has been valued for much longer than that. Why do we value gold so much?

As you'd know, we humans are successful because we collaborate. And to do so, we exchange goods and services – the barter system. You have rice, I have milk. I need rice, you need milk. We exchange and both walk away happy. But that still makes it difficult. What if I don't find someone to exchange milk with? The milk will rot the next day so I must give the milk to someone before it rots. If I wanted to keep the milk to buy something tomorrow, it would be difficult. So we need something to store our 'buying power' in. This is why gold was loved. Gold doesn't rot in one day. And over a period of time, humans learned that gold actually doesn't rot across hundreds of years. So I'd go exchange milk for some gold (I'd sell milk) and get gold coins. These gold coins, I could use any time I wished to. Gold is a store of buying power.

Why not any other metal like steel, copper or aluminium? They tend to rot over time due to corrosion. Across civilisations spanning thousands of years, gold has been used as a method of storing value. But it must be noted, only 35 per cent of gold is in the form of investment. Around 50 per cent is in the form of jewellery. All major civilisations have used gold as jewellery. The beauty of gold is that despite being made into jewellery, the value of gold isn't lost. It doesn't get 'used up'. If you cut paper and make ornaments out of it, it cannot be made back into sheets of paper. You can always get back your gold. Jewellery has become a status symbol over the years. Status symbol games are something that's deeply entrenched in our psyche. Gold jewellery helps us play that status symbol game – while at the same time, storing our wealth.

Eventually, people started storing gold in banks to keep it safe. And as proof of storage, the banks gave the people a certificate saying they had gold stored in the bank. Once this practice became common enough, people started exchanging certificates instead of the gold itself – that is how money notes came into circulation.

That's all good. But still, why is gold valued so much? About 800 years ago, fishermen in Russia discovered they could eat the eggs of a fish called sturgeon after some processes were performed. This is now famous as caviar. Nobody quite wanted it – it was food for the peasants. Somewhere along the line, a Russian Tsar fancied its taste and started having it regularly. Word spread, and more people wanted it. The problem was it took about eight years for the sturgeon fish to be ready with the eggs. There just weren't enough fish to go around. Caviar became rare and a status symbol – it remains one today. This helps us understand gold's rarity.

Gold is valuable because it is very durable and rare. Palladium is a metal that is even more durable than gold and even rarer. Why isn't it priced as high? It is so rare that one can barely find it. Nor is it as beautiful to look at. Gold has that perfect balance between being rare, being durable and being beautiful.

No matter the civilisation, people understand gold and will accept it as currency. It is argued that gold never really loses value. It never stops being a store of buying power. The buying power of the US dollar, Indian rupee, Japanese yen and all other currencies changes from time to time. It is argued that gold's value never changes.[1] That the amount of goods you could buy for 1 gram of gold 1,000 years ago is roughly the same as it is today. While the price of 1 gram of gold has changed, the price of the same quantity of goods has also changed similarly. This is why gold is viewed as a hedge against inflation. The belief is, if all else fails, gold will still have value.

Why does gold have value? Because of the above reasons, we humans collectively decide and agree that it has value. And therefore, it has value. And gold having value is one of the very few things that we all agreed on for thousands of years.

58

Avoid the Big Losses

WHILE RIDING IN A cab on your way to the office, which problem would you like your driver to focus more on? The AC not working or driving without crashing? Both are problems that affect you and must be addressed. But your driver's attention is limited. So you'd rather have them focus more on driving and less on the non-functional AC. With the AC not working, you might sweat and reach the office a bit untidy. With poor driving, you might not reach the office at all. In simple terms, this is risk management. The greatest risk needs to be addressed first and then the next greatest and then the next.

You will often hear some of the greatest investors say, 'The future cannot be predicted.' Most new investors tend to think that if a certain money manager cannot predict the future, why should they be trusted with money at all? We cannot predict the future. We can prepare ourselves for the future in the present. We can prepare in such a manner that if something good happens, we benefit from it, and if something bad happens, we suffer the least from it.

Investment is risk management, not predicting the future. Universa Investments is a hedge fund run by Mark Spitznagel.

In March 2020, the WHO declared that the world was in a pandemic. Flights all over the world stopped, everybody locked down and stayed home, businesses were shut, factories scaled down and a sense of economic gloom enveloped the world. The markets plummeted by 30–40 per cent worldwide. Mutual fund returns for many investors were down by over 50 per cent. But Universa's fund gave a return of over 3,600 per cent in March 2020. How?

Mark says his strategy isn't to predict the future but to manage risk. In March 2020, his risk management showed results. Every investor investing their own money in stocks, and every money manager, has one goal: to generate returns higher than the index. Whatever that index may be – Sensex, Dow Jones or any other. The entire point of investing in stocks yourself or giving money to a money manager to manage your investments is to make returns higher than the index. Because if the returns are lower than the index, what's the point in putting in all the effort and time?

Most investors and money managers adopt strategies to buy stocks in such a manner that the returns produced are higher than the index. At Universa, they do things a bit differently. Around 97 per cent of their assets are invested in the Standard and Poor's 500 (S&P 500) index. That's almost all of it. Why do investors bother giving their money to Universa? Because of how they manage the remaining 3 per cent of the assets.

For a long time, Universa delivered returns a bit lower than the index – which makes them seem not very useful, but this was done by design. Most cars have an extra wheel, a spare. One wheel by itself weighs quite a few kilograms, more weight means more fuel consumption.

Over a few years, imagine how much less fuel would be burnt if you had to carry about 10–15 kilograms less in weight. But you still carry the spare wheel. If, in an empty area, a tyre gets punctured and you do not have a spare wheel, arranging for transport to your destination will end up costing much more. Many people never have a punctured tyre but carry a spare wheel nonetheless. This in turn results in burning a little extra fuel – a cost they're willing to pay to avoid the greater risk of paying a lot more in cabs and puncture repair in deserted areas. Universa follows a similar philosophy. They're willing to lose some money regularly to ensure that when things go very wrong, they barely lose anything.

Universa invests around 97 per cent of the money in the S&P 500. And the remaining 3 per cent, they invest in puts. Of course, it isn't so simple. The true strategies of using puts to generate such high returns are trade secrets that Mark Spitznagel has not revealed. But what he's doing is managing risk. Different investors manage risk differently. Mark Spitznagel uses put options. Some money managers keep some reserve cash in bonds to deploy when the markets fall. Some make sure they're mostly invested in gold while investing the rest in very risky assets.

Many treat FDs as a safe haven for emergency or backup money. Investing is not predicting but managing risk. How are you managing your risk?

59

Evolve or Die

TAKE A LOOK AT the colour of lions. They blend in with their surroundings, ambush their prey and pounce on their target once they're close enough. Their colour blends well with the dry grass around them. It is said, 'Lions evolved to be a yellowish colour.' It may seem like lions as a species had a choice of colour and chose the right colour. This is obviously not true.

What happened is, through genetic mutations, some early lions would have had grass-like colour patches on their skin. These lions, because of their ability to camouflage and hunt better, were more successful in hunting. Therefore, they'd be healthier, mate often and have more cubs.

FIGURE 59.1 Lion depicting adaptive evolution and species survival

Eventually, from among the cubs, the ones who were even more grass-like in colour would continue to survive and pass on their genes, while the ones with a less favourable colour would eventually die of hunger. Over multiple generations, all the lions that survived would be of a grass-like colour. It isn't necessary that the lion that was the strongest survived. The lion that fit its surroundings the best survived. This is what experts term survival of the fittest. Those who fit their environment the best survive.

If tomorrow, all the grass around the lions turned brown or blackish, over hundreds of years, you'd find that the lions evolve to become browner or blackish. The shark we see today has barely evolved over millions of years because its environment has remained the same throughout that time. Individuals die fast but species survive for much longer. Every species aims to survive for as long as possible. This analogy can be drawn down to businesses very comfortably.

Over the course of a few decades, almost all the people working in any company would be gone and new ones would join. In effect, the company is comprised of almost entirely new people, but the company remains the same. This is because the company isn't just the people who work there. It is how those people interact with each other. These interactions can be anything from the rules governing the company to the culture within it. A company or business is like a species. Individuals come and go. The species remains for much longer.

Animals do go extinct. Entire species get wiped out. Animals have been going extinct when they failed to adapt to changing environments. Likewise, the environment of companies changes with time. The change in the case of species happens over thousands of years while the change in the case of companies can happen in merely a couple of years. But the analogy still holds. Sabre-tooth cats – animals like lions but much larger – went extinct around 10,000 years ago when a few other large animals they hunted went extinct due to climate change. They didn't like hunting smaller animals.

There's one difference between the changes in lions and those in the company. Lions don't have a choice about the changes they undergo as a species. While in a company, people have a choice as to how they evolve with the changing times. The Tata Group, as a company, is alive today and thriving over 150 years after it was founded. It started off as a trading company. At one point, its main business was textiles.

In the early 1900s, it started a steel company, a hotel company and an airline. Somewhere in the middle of the 1900s, Tata Motors was established. They started by making train engines. Towards the end of the 1900s, there were so many companies under Tata that it was hard to keep track. They made everything from trucks to salt.

How does Tata make the most money today? This 150-year-old company makes the most money out of something absolutely new-age: software. Tata Consultancy Services (TCS) is the biggest money-earner for Tata right now.

Over a 150-year period, the lion that Tata is today has changed colours many times to fit with the times and the environment. There are several others that perished in between because they failed to evolve.

Are you noticing how the Reliance Group is evolving right now? They're reducing their dependence on oil. They're investing massively and are already very big in the communications space (Jio) and retail space (Reliance Retail).

State Bank of India is even older than Tata, over 200 years old. It was a bank back then, and it is a bank even today. It operates in an environment where things haven't changed much. Similar to the sharks that did not need to evolve. The concept of a species evolving with changing environments doesn't apply only to companies. It applies to investors as well.

There was a time when investing in companies that didn't pay dividends was considered a poor move. Today, if an investor stuck to that philosophy, they would miss out on some of the best stocks. There was a time when any company with a PE ratio above twenty or thirty was deemed to be overvalued. Today, some of the best-performing stocks' PE ratios barely ever go below twenty. Times change. The fittest evolve and survive. Identify what it takes to be fit.

60

Are You Reading Through Your IPO?

In early 2019, WeWork was valued at over $47 billion. There were barely any other startups valued as much as it was. WeWork was started in 2010 by Adam Neumann. He had rented an office space for his own company, and he rented out a part of it to other people to save some rent. This is how he came up with the business idea for WeWork.

Right after the 2008 recession, many office spaces were empty in New York and there were no large companies willing to lease them out. WeWork started leasing these buildings, renovating them and offering them to individuals and companies on a per-table basis. WeWork was a co-working office space company.

Their spaces were a runaway hit. The interiors didn't look like traditional offices but like snazzy cafes. The company got many investors to back them. Sitting on a huge amount of money, the company started expanding and leasing out new office spaces to convert into WeWork co-working spaces. By 2010, this company was valued at over $10 billion.

WeWork offices opened up across different places in the world — including India. The per-desk cost at these co-working spaces was not as expensive as many might assume. When asked about his company in interviews, Adam Neumann didn't call WeWork a real estate company but presented it as a collaboration company. He insisted that the environment offered by WeWork was unmatched and led to great collaboration which couldn't be put into words.

From then on, Adam's personality and WeWork's offering attracted more startup entrepreneurs to shift their offices to WeWork. It seemed like the company was doing fantastic. In 2017, SoftBank, one of the biggest startup investors in the world, invested in the company valuing it at $20 billion.[1] That valuation was astronomical. SoftBank, to give you some idea, is one of the biggest startup investors in the world at present.

Even in India, some of the biggest startup names have received funding from SoftBank. SoftBank continued to invest in the company. With each successive round, the valuation of the company rose further. As WeWork was a private company, nobody knew how it was growing so fast and valued at such a high amount. If the company was indeed growing so fast and expanding its revenue, more investors would want to get on board and invest in it.

The company announced its plans to go for an IPO in September 2019. To go for an IPO, a company has to make many details public for investors to see. WeWork did that. The first metric that wasn't surprising was that WeWork wasn't profitable. It was losing money. However, that is common among many startups that are expanding to grow fast. It was entirely possible that WeWork would become profitable in the future. The next set of numbers boggled investors.

The total square footage of space WeWork had, the total number of users, total locations and revenue were all either similar to or lower than those of another publicly listed company called International Workplace Group (IWG). IWG was an older company doing the exact same task; it was profitable and was valued at around $4 billion.

Why was WeWork valued so much? Upon closer inspection, it was clear that the company was overvalued by too much. Additionally, it came to light that Adam was profiteering from the company. He rented spaces in his own name and then rented them back to WeWork at much higher prices. There were more examples of such behaviour. Investors who were curious to invest in WeWork's IPO pulled away from it. WeWork cancelled its IPO and cut its valuation by over 80 per cent. Adam Neumann was fired. Eventually, a new CEO was hired whose aim was to make the company profitable. Mass layoffs happened and many WeWork locations shut down.

The backlash received from Wall Street caused the company to cancel its IPO in September 2019 because investors had read through the details of the company's records when it filed for an IPO. Are you reading through the records of the IPOs you are investing in?

61

Factory of the World

A FEW YEARS AGO, there was an internet forward circulating on WhatsApp. It showed an astronaut standing on the surface of the moon holding an American flag. Beside that image was a close-up zoom of the flag held by the astronaut. On the American flag were tiny letters that said, 'Made in China'. It is not fully known if that forward was indeed true or not. But the message of that internet forward or meme was clear – China seems to make everything. China is the factory of the world. Even in the case of items that are manufactured in other countries, more often than not, there will be raw materials or components that came from a factory in China.

Towards the middle of the 1900s, China was a nation that had a massive population which was poor and depended heavily on agriculture. After the ruins of the Second World War, East Asian countries like Japan, South Korea and Taiwan had adopted Western economic systems. In just a few decades, these countries had gone from being agriculture-dependent economies to modern, export-driven economies. The manufacturing of electronics was a major driver for these nations. Towards the 1970s, China realised that depending on agriculture alone wasn't going to help the country's economy. They had a massive population that was young and growing every year. This meant that there were many young, capable hands to do vast amounts of work but not enough jobs. Due to this reason, the salaries they wanted were very low as there was immense competition.

As a country, the way China operates is different from many others. China is very centralised in its approach. The government has greater power and control over policies, so planned changes or reforms can be executed faster than in most other countries. China encouraged the setting up of factories for simple articles that didn't require immense technical knowledge. Soon, attracted by the cheap labour costs in the country, many foreign brands started setting up factories for their simple goods. The factory workers were able to earn better wages than those working on the farms.

A massive shift began over a few years. People started leaving their farms behind and moving to urban areas in search of better jobs, resulting in the availability of cheap labour. More companies found it cheaper to manufacture in China. As more companies set up factories in China, they realised that with a little bit of training, the young Chinese workforce could make more advanced goods. This was a constant cycle. Over the years, the Chinese workforce kept getting better and better. There was a time when Chinese-manufactured goods stood for low-quality and inexpensive items. Today, no piece of advanced technology can be made without using at least some parts made in China, often critical parts.

This sounds easy for governments to do but it isn't. Setting up a factory in China was incredibly easy, unlike in most other countries. Permissions, construction, electricity supply, everything happened fast with the government's watchful eye. Manufacturing in China was so easy, nearly every major company moved there and trained the workforce. Not just that, China ensured the setting up of Special Economic Zones (SEZs). These SEZs had facilities to encourage manufacturing in every way. The country made huge ports for export ships to load up, and excellent highways and rail networks to move goods from factories to ports. For manufacturing, China was an extremely appealing location to set up a factory.

By the 1990s, in just around fifteen or twenty years of adopting this change, China was making everything. At the same time, their population was growing at an incredible pace. The government introduced another law to control this worry of theirs: the one-child policy. This worked and the population stopped growing as fast. To continue moving its citizens from poverty to the middle class, China took many measures to ensure continued economic growth. New massive cities were built, businesses were encouraged and education was paramount. Growth was prioritised over everything else. In 2001, nearly two-thirds of all trade in the world was happening with the US. By 2018, it was happening with China.

Today, China is the world's second-largest economy behind only the US. In 2021, the US's GDP was around $22 trillion. China's GDP was around $18 trillion. To continue this growth, China cannot continue depending on exports alone. It is trying to utilise its own consumption from a growing middle class to ensure continued economic growth. At the same time, its population has started ageing. The earlier introduced one-child policy has led to a drastic reduction in the population of the young. China tried to encourage population growth by introducing a three-child policy. With wages climbing, manufacturing in China is getting more expensive, this is one reason why many manufacturers are trying to move to other countries.

China's central style of operation is largely believed to be the reason why it has prospered so quickly. It doesn't take them time to implement new changes. But then, many question if that kind of control and the accompanying loss of individual freedom is worth the economic growth.

What the future holds for China is impossible to predict. These are the challenges every nation wanting to become a manufacturing hub faces and everybody is solving these issues using different methods.

62

When Geniuses Got Together

John Meriwether was a bond trader at Salomon Brothers – an investment bank. What made him different was that he had a knack for tracking and convincing talent. He had developed what can be described as an underground network that had its roots deep in the academic world.

John personally knew the best professors and students across some of the most prestigious universities in America. He had convinced many of them to quit their academic jobs and move to the world of high finance. Using this network, he had hired traders at Salomon Brothers.

In 1991, Salomon was caught in a treasury securities fraud, the blame for which landed on John Meriwether. He paid a fine and left Salomon Brothers. Once he quit, many of the talents he had hired at Salomon Brothers also started to quit the investment bank. In 1993, he announced his own hedge fund – Long Term Capital Management (LTCM).

John had two other big names with him. Myron Scholes and Robert Merton. Their entire team was filled with smart, top-of-the-line people. A news article wrote that their office had the highest density of IQ points per square foot anywhere in the world.[1] In 1994, LTCM formally opened its doors, and from day one, it was making unheard-of returns. Being a hedge fund, the regulations applied to it were very minimal, unlike those applied to a mutual fund.

LTCM's secret strategy was in arbitrage. LTCM called itself a financial-technology company. These complex and intricate mathematical models were used by their high-technology computers to trade. The hedge fund was so prestigious, even before they launched, that it attracted many huge investors like CEOs, heads of banks, pension funds and sovereign funds.

As anyone else would expect, right from the moment they started, they were stellar. In their first year, they earned over 20 per cent. In 1995, 43 per cent; in 1996, they earned 41 per cent. This small bunch of traders had more in profits than some of the biggest brands in the world. But the world of finance has some crazy-smart people working in it. It is a game where very smart people are playing against other very smart people. Soon, other hedge funds were able to replicate LTCM's strategy.

Gradually, the size of opportunities available to LTCM shrunk. Unable to make gargantuan returns, they decided to return $2.7 billion to the original investors which was still a good amount. LTCM would make huge profits by using leverage. They'd borrow money and invest in order to be able to make huge amounts of money.

Banks didn't have a problem lending to them due to their track record. When LTCM returned the money to its original investors, it didn't take down its position sizes. In short, the money they had borrowed was much larger than the amount they had with them. They calculated that the risk of something going wrong was something they could take. And the calculation of risk was a skill nobody doubted.

According to their calculation, the most they could have lost was $35 million. The economic situation was such that things started to spiral down. In 1998, within a few months, they had lost $1.9 billion, far more than the $35 million they had originally calculated. The losses were so big, LTCM's position threatened to cause a global economic collapse. The Fed had to bail them out.

Many of their biggest investors lost their entire investments. LTCM's spokesperson once famously said, 'Risk is a function of volatility. These things are quantifiable.'[2] They believed they could calculate the probability of events and quantify risk, but their models failed in the real world.

Famous author Nassim Taleb said about them, 'They made absolutely no allowance in the episode of LTCM for the possibility of their not understanding markets and their methods being wrong.'[3] Nassim is someone who believes humans cannot calculate the probability of big events. Experts, no matter how good they are, can be wrong when it comes to prediction. Newton, one of the smartest scientists to have ever lived, is famous for having lost money in the stock markets and saying, 'I can calculate the motions of heavenly bodies, but not the madness of the people.'[4]

63

How Did It Start?

SOME YEARS AGO, Amsterdam was the hub of global finance. Companies dealing with many parts of the world would come to Amsterdam to seek financing, to trade, to exchange and to look for business partnerships. We have already explained how the stock markets were born in this part of the world. There was an owner of a brokerage office in Amsterdam in the late 1700s named Abraham van Ketwich.

In 1772, there was a stock market crash that led to many deep losses. These investment losses were in the bonds of companies. The smaller investors were worse hit because they were either investing in bonds of only one company or a very small number of companies. Large investors had enough cash to invest in all kinds of companies and they invested in only one. Ketwich, who was the owner of a brokerage office, came up with a method to help these smaller investors. The problem for the investors was simply that they didn't have enough money to invest in the bonds of multiple companies.

Ketwich collected money from several small investors and amassed a large amount which he invested in the bonds of several companies. In effect, all small investors became investors in bonds of several companies, and the risk was spread out. This is referred to as diversification. Ketwich called this 'Negotiatie', which stands for 'strength in unity'. This is how the concept for the world's first mutual fund was born – even though it wasn't called a mutual fund. The idea behind a mutual fund is mostly this: investors' money is pooled and invested. That is exactly what Ketwich did.

In the case of Ketwich, the main intention was to achieve diversification. Another objective may be to let an expert with deep knowledge invest your money for you. The fund Ketwich created didn't last too long, but the idea spread. In the late 1890s, the idea reached the US. The Boston Personal Property Trust was started with the intention of pooling money from investors and investing in real estate. Till this point, the funds were mostly close-ended in nature. This means investors could only take out money at some intervals.

In 1907, a fund named the Alexander Fund in the US allowed investors to withdraw money whenever they wished – they were open-ended in nature. This is more like modern-day mutual funds that we are used to. In 1924, the first modern-day mutual fund was born. It was called MFS Massachusetts Investors Trust, and it had State Street Investor's Trust as its custodian. This changed everything. Mutual funds started having custodians. Until this point, investors gave their money to mutual funds, and they did everything. In the custodian concept, a mutual fund company has only the right to manage the money; it doesn't actually have the money.

The actual money and assets are held and kept secure by another reputed company called the custodian. Every mutual fund, even in India, has a custodian which is not the mutual fund company itself. In 1929, a fund called Wellington Fund was introduced. Believe it or not, this fund is still around today. In the 1930s, the Great Depression hit and the public's interest in the stock markets started fading. The twenty or thirty years after that were not so remarkable for the markets and therefore, by extension, for the mutual funds. Things started looking up towards the mid-1900s. Newer mutual funds were launched in the US. More people started investing in the stock markets.

Additionally, many investors started liking the idea of an expert investing in the stock markets for them. Hence, mutual funds rose in popularity. Some good mutual funds delivered returns much higher than most investors managed to get from the stock markets. Over the years, some funds managed to give these very high returns for extended periods of time. The names of these funds and their managers became household names in America; one such name is Peter Lynch. His ideas and teachings are now famous with investors all over the world. Investors were of course investing in these funds to gain from the fund manager's expertise and not merely to diversify.

A huge chunk of the American working class was investing in mutual funds. Around the same time, the very first Indian mutual fund was born. Unit Trust of India (UTI) was established in 1964. By the late 1980s, UTI was managing over ₹6,000 crore of investors' money. Towards the end of the 1900s and the start of the 2000s, newer kinds of funds were born. In India, they were still a new concept. In the 1990s, a few other public sector mutual fund companies also got in the game – LIC, SBI, GIC and a few others. In the 2000s, private mutual fund companies started business in India too.

By this point, mutual funds had become largely the kind we know today. They are immensely regulated and watched closely by the industry watchdogs, SEBI in India and the SEC in the US. In 2008, the Great Recession hit the world, but the popularity of mutual funds as investment options didn't suffer too much. But in the US, this did bring about a fundamental change. Investors started shifting from mutual funds managed by fund managers to index funds and Exchange Traded Funds (ETFs) that were not actively managed by any fund manager but tracked some index automatically. Basically, the move was from actively managed funds to passively managed funds.

This move made sense since, in the US, index-tracking funds and ETFs were giving better returns. In India, the same has not been true so far. There are a good number of mutual funds that have given higher returns than index funds and ETFs. But there is a massive difference between the US and India. In the US, around 40–50 per cent of the population invests in mutual funds of some sort. In India, that number was 3–4 per cent. Until about 2013–14, most mutual fund investors in India were from urban areas.

Things started changing with the spread of cheap internet and smartphones across the country, and many investment apps came in. We were one of them back in 2016. The first version of the 'Groww Digest' was also started then. But the percentage of the Indian population that invests in stocks or mutual funds is very small, only about 7 per cent. In fact, Indian investors aren't able to enjoy the much higher returns they could because many aren't even aware that they don't have to pick stocks themselves and can opt for mutual funds where a fund manager make the decisions. Anyway, if you noticed, the mutual funds of today have much the same intention that was behind the very birth of mutual funds – offering diversification and access to expert fund managers to smaller investors. Technology is changing how funds work, but at the end of the day, the only funds that have survived so far and will survive in the future are the ones that benefit their investors.

64

What Happened in 1991?

BPL TV. Bajaj Chetak. MTNL phone. HM Ambassador. What do these remind you of? Someone in your family? Someone who is slightly older? Sony music system. Ford Cortina. Samsung fridge. Do these remind you of the same person? Obviously not because these items were never sold in India in the same era. What changed: the Licence Raj era.

After Indian Independence, the Indian government had made a structure that kept tight control over the industries operating in India. This was done to manage resources well – remember, India was a very poor and under-resourced nation in the 1950s. This control of the government was through licences and permits. An incredibly high number of permits and licences were required to set up new businesses. The rules for foreign companies operating in India were very stringent. For example, they required government permission to operate in India and were often allowed in a manner where they had to set up a joint venture with an Indian company.

Rules also forbade international companies from owning more than 40 per cent of an Indian company. How this tight government control worked for India is a matter of long discussion. Some believe it was necessary at that point in time, while some say we could have benefited more without it. But in the 1980s, this very control became extremely problematic because corruption was rampant.

The procedures were elaborate, resulting in very few international companies in India. Very few world-class companies operated in India, and a quality workforce was never cultivated. Some of the leading countries that produce high-quality goods learned from other nations' practices. Japan, South Korea and China are the best examples.

Economic Crisis 1991

India was barely producing goods that were export-worthy. India had good trade relations with the USSR. With the USSR, India had trade relations in rupees. Most of the world treated the US dollar as the international trade currency. If India wanted to buy something from France, it would have to pay in US dollars. And if France wanted to buy something from India, it would have to pay in rupees. Since India was producing very few goods, it did not export much to other nations.

At the same time, India was importing many goods because it couldn't make them. One of our biggest imports was crude oil without which nothing would work. Barely any exports and very high imports meant that the number of dollars (trade balance) reduced rapidly. The USSR collapsed around the same time and the Gulf War started in this period. This meant two things: one of our biggest trade partners was no longer importing from us and oil became very expensive. Both were horrible news for our trade balance.

In 1991, we had a trade balance that would last only two weeks. This was a full-blown economic crisis. Inflation was in double digits and unemployment was extremely high. Our fiscal deficit was ballooning. India went to the International Monetary Fund (IMF) to seek loans to fund itself. After millions of people had died in the war, nobody wanted another war. If countries trade and do business with each other, they won't try to kill each other because they depend on each other. This was the idea many had in their minds back then.

The IMF was established to facilitate this very thought. When India approached the IMF for a loan, the IMF would give money. Whenever the IMF gives money to nations, it has a few conditions. One of those conditions was to ensure more trade and business among nations. It asked India to open up its economy which resulted in the liberalisation of 1991. The central government that year was extremely unstable. P.V. Narasimha Rao was a new prime minister, along with Manmohan Singh, the finance minister. On 24 July 1991, the finance minister presented the budget.

Singh announced sweeping reforms including the conditions that the IMF wished for: abolishing the Licence Raj. From having licensing restrictions on all industries, India went to removing all licences except in eighteen security-related industries. Foreign companies were welcomed to set up business in India with ownership of up to 51 per cent. Additionally import duties were reduced. While presenting the budget, the finance minister also said the following lines: 'But as Victor Hugo once said, no power on earth can stop an idea whose time has come. I suggest to this august House that the emergence of India as a major economic power in the world happens to be one such idea ...'[1]

What followed was the rise of the Indian economy. Over thirty years later, India has now become the world's sixth-largest economy. India's forex reserves are more than $500 billion strong; it was around $5 billion in 1990. New companies started selling products in India. Many started setting up factories in India. Samsung, Hyundai, McDonald's and Nokia among many others. These factories led to the development of local talent and technological prowess as more Indians learned important skills firsthand, resulting in large-scale employment.

Liberalisation did not completely open up the country. India continues to have many bottlenecks. But that day marked the day when India started removing those bottlenecks. Governments that have come after that day continue to increase Foreign Direct Investment (FDI) limits and reduce the number of permits and licences required. The 1991 liberalisation was far more nuanced, and books like *To the Brink and Back* and *1991: How P.V. Narasimha Rao Made History* discuss the concept in great detail.

65

Making No Mistakes

BILL ACKMAN IS AN investor who is much praised and is often referred to as the next Warren Buffett. At a talk at Oxford University, he discussed the importance of making mistakes. He mentioned how he thinks the students at Oxford, being young and academically successful, hadn't made enough mistakes yet. Bill also spoke about his experience with JCPenney.

Retail chains in the US are struggling today as people don't shop as much as before in stores. The rise of e-commerce companies like Amazon means that a vast number of people prefer to order online, but that doesn't necessarily mean it is the end of the road for them. Shopping remains an experience even today. Before buying a shirt, shoe or perfume, people like to touch and feel what they're spending money on

Many people like the experience of being in a physical store, of catching a good discount, of spending a day looking for the perfect dress. If this weren't the case, existing retail outlets would have converted to online sales and shut down their physical stores altogether. But it is still a struggling space. JCPenney is one such chain in the US. It was founded in 1902 with one store. The company was known for its values.

J.C. Penney was the name of the founder of the chain – he was a man of strong values. Penny worked only in cash and avoided credit because he believed credit could ruin his merchants. Penney wished to offer a good deal to his customers and priced goods at his store accordingly. The company's growth accelerated as it was a hit among customers. In 1928, it crossed 1,000 stores across the US.

By the 1950s, it was a retail giant and sold a wide variety of goods from clothes and apparel to high-end fashion. It soon made its way to shopping malls after being an independent store chain. By the 2000s, the company started struggling as its founder had died a couple of decades earlier and JCPenney saw a string of CEOs get hired and leave within a few years. The 2008 recession worsened the situation, making the middle class spend less money.

In 2010, Bill Ackman bought a 16.5 per cent stake in the company and became a board member. He wished to turn the company around. As an activist investor, his plan was simple; he'd take control of the company, hire the right people and steer the company out of the place it was in. The brand was iconically American and had a lot of promise. That would result in the company making a good profit and his shares' price climbing.

Ron Johnson

When JCPenney's board met to discuss who the next best CEO for the company would be, one name kept coming up: Ron Johnson. Ron had studied at Harvard University before going to work at Target, one of America's most successful department stores. He worked there for over a decade until he was hired by Steve Jobs to work at Apple. What would a department store executive help Apple with? Apple stores.

We don't have Apple stores in India yet but they're a big thing in the US. It is an experience. People line up outside stores to buy their favourite devices when they are newly launched. These stores look extremely suave, clean, minimalist and yet warm. There aren't many items on display except for the few gadgets that Apple sells and the focus of the stores is to get visitors to touch and use the products.

Ron was the man behind these stores. He was convinced to leave Apple and was hired by JCPenney to be the CEO of the company. Ron was quick to look at JCPenney's sheets and identify where money was getting wasted and mobilise idle assets. Then, he introduced his grand plan. Until then, JCPenney would launch a product at a certain price, and almost nobody bought at this price.

The company introduced around a 50 per cent discount and sales started taking place. They later introduced discount coupons at 50 per cent – at this price, most of the items got sold. Ron found this a waste of time. He designed a seamless system where the items would be priced very low from the start – the price at which they sold after multiple discounts.

He convinced many brands to open mini-stores within the JCPenney stores – brands that would have otherwise avoided being at JCPenney. He designed a seamless experience where customers would pay electronically only at the end of their shopping. This new system sounded brilliant. It was rolled out across the country, but it failed. JCPenney's customers had gotten accustomed to buying using discount coupons.

Without the coupons, the customers didn't buy anything, even though the prices were low from the start. JCPenney lost a huge chunk of customers in this endeavour. Most stores when they roll out a new scheme or experience usually test it in a small region and then expand it to all their stores. Apple worked differently. Steve Jobs's philosophy was more akin to 'We understand what the user needs better'.

That philosophy worked for Apple as they were inventing new experiences for their customers, so they didn't test it and just rolled out new schemes. That wasn't the case with JCPenney. But Ron Johnson was used to rolling out changes in one go. After this failure, Ron Johnson had to leave JCPenney. Bill Ackman talks of this event as one of his biggest failures.

Ackman argues this wouldn't have happened if Ron had experienced more failures in his life. He goes on to say he believes Ron is a better executive today because of his failures. Bill Ackman emphasises how important it is to make small failures. He himself describes his investing career so far as a mixed bag of failures and successes – the successes are bigger than his failures.

66

Markets and Wars

HE CANNOT AFFORD TO move out from here, and besides, this is his home so why should he leave? He has a family of four to feed and take care of. He used to sell vegetables but now there's barely any produce growing, nor are there many buyers. There are very few jobs and rival armies fight each other, often killing civilians. News of the death of friends and family is common.

This description is not of any one person in a particular geographic location. This is pretty much how people live in war zones. Today global trade is so widespread, and our economies are connected in ways many of us fail to imagine. The news is filled with reports of the Russia–Ukraine conflict. The day the conflict started, the Russian markets tanked by around 50 per cent.[1]

The markets were shut following that and remained shut for a few days. Sanctions were put on Russia by many countries to discourage them, which means there are limits to the trade companies and countries can carry out with Russia. The sanctions this time are some of the most stringent. Russia, like most other nations, relies on imports and exports for its economy to function.

With so many sanctions, very little international trade is possible for Russians. Imported goods are running out of stock. Prices are climbing sky-high. The exchange rate of the Russian currency has fallen so much, it is impossibly expensive to buy things that were affordable just days ago. At present, the uncertainty is such, it is hard to tell when things will get easier for the Russians.

The conditions were worse in Ukraine. People fled their homes to escape the war. Either that or they're fighting in the war. The economies of the two nations are extremely bad; this is just the economy. The loss in terms of life is far worse. Needless to say, with such a condition of both countries' economies, the immediate future doesn't look very bright for them.

But why have the rest of the globe's markets fallen in the same period? This is because the economies of the world are connected – we're all trading with each other. Russian gas powers great parts of Europe. Russian oil is exported all around the world. So, if things get tough there, the prices go up. Every time energy prices go up, the prices of everything go up. When prices go up in one part of the world, it has repercussions in other parts.

If you want to measure the cost to the economy, try to measure the disruption any event has on the economy. Any event – not just wars. The pandemic was a disruption. Natural calamities can be disruptions. A small war might cause disruption, but it'll be minor in nature. So not much effect. A large war might cause greater disruption hence a greater effect on the economy. A multi-country war would cause so much disruption, it'd be hard to not be affected – hence it would almost certainly affect us all.

Though it must be noted, wars have been surprisingly less heavy on the stock markets. The US stock markets actually grew during the two world wars. Something similar happened during the Vietnam War. More recently, the US was in a war with Iraq, but it didn't affect the global markets as much. Russia annexed Crimea in 2014 – that hasn't left any lasting impact on the markets. In India, a war did happen in recent times – the Kargil War.

It didn't have much effect on the markets in hindsight. The economic disruption caused by it wasn't big. What we do see is that when a war breaks out, or when there are fears of a war breaking out, the markets tend to fall amid the panic. A very recent example is that of the India–Pakistan tension in 2019. It didn't escalate into a war, but it did spook the markets for a few days in February 2019.

In the past, too, major markets have been temporarily worried when a conflict started. But in the longer run, they've recovered just fine. Right now, the volatility in the markets is because we don't know how long the Ukraine–Russia conflict will last; we don't know if it'll remain between those two countries or if it'll escalate beyond them; we don't know how much disruption to the globe it'll cause. Nobody knows the future.

We all can agree on one thing beyond the economic effects of wars – the loss of lives on all sides is not worth it. History tells us that more often than not, the markets do okay. But then, history is also an account of things that never happened before.

67

Asian Fish in American Waters

FISH FARMERS HATE ALGAE. They hate many other kinds of rapid vegetation found in water. Too many algae and vegetation can limit the number of fish that can be produced in water. Too much of it can completely wipe out all the fish. Putting chemicals in the water to kill these types of vegetation leads to more harm than good.

In the 1960s, scientists in Arkansas chanced upon a brilliant idea. No chemicals, no pesticides and no artificial ingredients in aquatic life. In Eastern Asia – Korea, China – there's a fish called the Asian carp. It eats algae and water vegetation. There are many types of Asian carp, and a few of those are found in India too. Heard of the very commonly eaten fish called Rohu and Catla?

Some of these Asian carp were imported to Arkansas and kept in a few water bodies. Within days, the problems vanished. The water was clearer than it had ever been. Scientists studied the carp further. This was an aggressive species. It ate whatever came in its path and reproduced very fast. A small population of carp could easily grow very large, very fast. Also, in the American rivers, the fish had no natural prey. They knew this. They measured the pros and cons, and the pros offered by the carp (they kept the water clear of algae and vegetation) seemingly outweighed the cons.

Farmers in the southern US started importing more live Asian carp to keep in their water bodies. Carp weren't eaten but were used to keep waters clear to farm other fish. Their fish production grew and they were happy – this was the best way to keep their waters clean without using harmful chemicals.

The fish was supposed to be kept only in farming ponds and nowhere else; it was isolated from the natural waters of the country. As the news of the success of these fish spread, more farmers wanted them. Did the fish accidentally escape into the natural waters? Yes. Every few years, someone would randomly catch a carp in the rivers. But that was that. Only a few random catches here and there.

It is impossible to prevent fish from escaping into the rivers when so many farmers have them. But the few that had managed to escape into the rivers were only twenty or thirty at best. They seemingly posed no threat to the local fish species. Except, that was not the case. It was true that only a few fish had managed to escape into the rivers. But it was not true that they posed no threat.

In the 1990s, the US saw extreme flooding. When the floods receded and left many stranded dead fish behind, local scientists were stunned to find that nine out of the ten dead fish beside the rivers were Asian carp. They had practically wiped out the local fish species causing huge ecological damage. Over the years, the fish have spread to a majority of the states in the US.

Attempts to curb them have not been successful because they spread too fast. Attempts are made to kill them in massive numbers. There are competitions where the most catches are rewarded. These competitions have been happening for decades. However, they don't help dent the population of the fish one bit.

Most of the carp are as big as a cat or a small dog. Some are as big as a ten-year-old child. Some scientists are employing various types of new techniques to reduce the carp population and some of these techniques are working. But nothing on a large scale has come up so far. The early scientists and farmers were well aware of this nature of the fish.

The problem is the population increases so fast; it isn't intuitive for humans to understand. Two fish (mom and dad) result in hundreds more (children). So far, so good. But then those hundred children fish become a couple and each produces hundreds more. And that cycle continues. Compounding. We, humans, are very good at understanding small numbers like two and five, or maybe hundered. But beyond that, we need to think carefully or use pen and paper. Yes, many of us can perform mental math with high numbers but it still isn't intuitive — it requires deliberate thought. We don't have the intuition because the way our ancestors evolved, we never dealt with large numbers. Now give that human brain a very large number and you have a problem.

Hit that brain with two very large numbers that multiply, and you have an even bigger problem — a compounded problem. Understand that we humans don't have the intuitive sense to understand compounding. Hence, we always need to sit and think about things that compound carefully. Doing so can help us save ourselves from massive problems.

It wasn't that the scientists who measured the benefits and the disadvantages of the Asian carp didn't work hard, but they had not considered how fast compounding would take place. If we're better at understanding compounding, we can take advantage of compounding through things that are good for us. It would be nice if something we like grew as fast as the Asian carp population, we essentially mean money. Many investors fail to realise how their expenses will rise as the years go by, and they run after short-term gains and fail to realise the bigger gains they could have had from long-term investing.

68

How Does Russia's War Affect Petrol?

Elections were being held in five states of India just a few days ago. In another part of the world, Russia and Ukraine entered a massive conflict. Some people in the country started saying that the price of petrol and diesel was about to dramatically shoot up. And this wouldn't be a minor increase. It would be a ₹10 or so increase. Why was it so?

What causes the price of petrol and diesel to go up? What do Russia and Ukraine have to do with oil prices? And finally, why does it matter? Crude oil is a thick black liquid that has been known to us for hundreds of years. It naturally oozes out in some parts of the world where the earth's crust is relatively thin.

In the 1800s, when the Industrial Revolution resulted in modern-day machinery, we realised this thick black liquid was as important to modern life as oxygen. Of course, the little crude oil oozing out of the earth here and there wasn't enough and great effort was made to discover places to extract more of it.

Today, most of our oil comes from these deep oil wells that are constructed after discovering oil hundreds of meters below the surface. Some countries discovered they were sitting on massive amounts of crude oil while most others didn't have much oil under their soil. These handful of countries became obnoxiously rich exporting a resource the world desperately needs.

Oil prices are dictated by demand and supply. It's a giant global market. Every producer is trying to sell oil and every nation is trying to buy. Different countries try to produce more oil and outbid each other causing the prices to fall. This resulted in bad losses for the countries producing the oil as well as volatility in oil prices.

OPEC

OPEC stands for the Organization of Petroleum Exporting Countries. This organisation was formed back in the 1960s. There are thirteen countries in this organisation. Together, these countries produce 80 per cent of the world's oil. These are mostly countries in the Middle East and Africa. OPEC decides how much oil they will produce to keep prices at good levels (for themselves). The demand for oil also changes from time to time and OPEC adjusts its supply accordingly. For example, around 2014, they decided to keep supply at a level where they could keep the price around $100 per barrel. OPEC is often accused of being a cartel that keeps prices high enough to benefit itself – making it harder for oil-importing nations.

But plans don't always work out. There are countries that produce oil that aren't part of OPEC. The US has a lot of oil in the form of shale. This is oil embedded in rocks and not openly in liquid form like a regular oil well. In recent years, thanks to advancements in technology, taking out this shale oil became more viable.

In the mid-2010s, America started producing enough oil to disrupt the oil market. The excess production led to oil prices falling to around $60 per barrel. The amount of oil being pumped out by OPEC countries and non-OPEC countries is a major determinant of global crude oil prices. So far, we've seen that the amount of oil produced by OPEC countries and non-OPEC countries influences crude oil prices. This is basic supply and demand, and anything that affects supply and demand affects oil prices. There are some major themes in the disruption. Oil is produced in a handful of countries and everyone else uses it. How does the oil reach everybody else? Giant ships. And a few pipelines.

If there's a natural disaster that affects the ships' movement or the pipelines' condition, supply can fall massively (price increases). If there's a war or a conflict in an oil-producing country, it faces difficulty in operating its oil wells. Supply falls (price increases). In 2020, a different natural disaster happened – the COVID-19 pandemic. Lockdowns meant transport was largely stopped due to complete shutdown. Demand fell. There was enough supply but demand for oil fell (price decreases). Every time there is a war near a sea route where oil ships pass by the movement of oil-carrying ships is affected. Where do Russia and Ukraine fit in this? Russia is a major oil producer that isn't a member of OPEC. In recent years, its oil and gas have powered Europe to a large extent. With the war between Russia and Ukraine, there was fear that this oil production would be affected. Hence the prices shot astronomically high. Why does the price of oil matter so much? Because modern life without it isn't possible. It isn't just petrol you fill in your scooter or car. That's a smaller portion.

Practically everything that's transported – milk, rice, vegetables, medicines, computers, cement – gets transported on a vehicle that runs on diesel. You know how you can go to any part of the country and even if the electricity is down, your phone gets network? That's because there's a diesel generator powering the nearest cellular tower.

Diesel price goes up, and everything becomes more expensive. And diesel is made from crude oil. In India, the government decides the price of petrol and diesel.

The price of crude oil isn't allowed to directly impact the price of petrol and diesel. It is common to keep petrol and diesel prices stable during elections. So while the 2024 Lok Sabha elections were on, the prices of petrol and diesel didn't rise. When they were over, many expected the prices to climb. But by then, a number of oil-producing nations increased their supply in response to the disruption caused by the Russia–Ukraine conflict, and global crude oil prices started falling to older levels again.

69

When Your Gain Is Someone's Loss

A COUPLE OF YEARS AGO, the Indian market had several cellular providers offering 3G and 4G services. Back then, 1GB of data that would last about a month cost somewhere between ₹200 and ₹300. Towards the late 2000s and early 2010s, there was a massive pricing war. Companies were trying to undercut each other by offering cheaper rates. There were several players like Airtel, Idea, Tata, Vodafone, Aircel and BSNL. The executives in each company faced immense challenges in pricing their offerings because each company had a good network in urban and semi-urban areas. There was nothing to differentiate one company from the other except the price. Take Airtel, for example. If they wanted to appeal to more customers, they would have to reduce their prices, but if they reduced their pricing too much, it would reduce their profits. On the other side, let's say in Vodafone's office, their executive gets a hint that Airtel might be about to reduce their prices. To undercut them, Vodafone decides to reduce the price just enough to undercut Airtel's new lower price. Airtel knows that word spreads fast and that even Vodafone will try to reduce prices.

If Vodafone reduces prices too much, then Airtel gets no advantage by reducing its price. But keeping the price where it is means everybody starts moving to Vodafone and must reduce the price. Now, if you were working with Airtel, what would you do? This is a classic example of game theory.

When you are competing for a limited resource (in this case, mobile phone users), your gain is someone else's loss. And your loss is someone else's gain. This is called a zero-sum game, and the people you are competing against are intelligent and rational. What do you do?

In the example stated, it would be better for all companies to agree that it is harmful to them to continue fighting each other as well as to continue reducing the prices. Ideally, they would just agree to keep the prices where they were so that all of them could benefit. But each company wants more profits and they're not concerned about the well-being of the other. That's what sets off a pricing war benefitting the consumer. At one point, the companies reached a sort of stalemate – a place where they didn't want to reduce further. They weren't cooperating but they weren't fighting each other either. This is where the prices had stabilised.

This is called a Nash equilibrium. A new player entered the scene – someone who was willing to offer cheaper rates to gain customers. Jio was able to enter the space and offer 30 GB per month for ₹100 and ₹200. That was such a blow, many of those companies mentioned earlier didn't survive.

Those who did survive had to reduce prices to Jio's levels. Airtel did very well because they fought back with similarly lower prices. Since Jio entered, the total number of cellular companies operating in India went from twelve to only four. Game theory is a very real phenomenon. It plays out in every sphere of life – wars, politics, business, our personal relations ... everywhere.

To better understand the concept of Nash Equilibrium, we recommend reading about the 'Prisoner's Dilemma'. But in this case, there's an assumption. The assumption here is that the person you are fighting is also smart and is being rational. What makes every zero-sum game far more complicated is that the person you are against isn't necessarily being rational.

Then, it becomes difficult to predict what the other side might do. If you look at US presidents, they were expected to be rational. When US ex-president Donald Trump started a trade war with China, China was thrown off. In such interactions, it is believed that everyone wants to hurt the other while not hurting themselves.

The trade war was hurting China, but it was also hurting the US itself. Do you know where else game theory plays out? Yes, investing. At least in the short-term, investing has a huge component of game theory in it. This is why trading is so difficult but long-term investing is relatively easier. Trading is a zero-sum game. How you make money depends on what the other traders are thinking and planning. To add to that, you don't know how rational they are being. Maybe they're being very smart. Or maybe they're being very foolish. You have no clue. It is estimated that about 80–90 per cent of traders lose money. Only a few make money.

In long-term investing, the total pool of money or value increases so much that it isn't practically a zero-sum game. Game theory applies a lot less there. It isn't necessary for some investors to lose money for you to gain money.

70

The (Dis)Advantages of Being Big

ARNOLD SCHWARZENEGGER, THE AUSTRIAN bodybuilder, came to the US and worked incredibly hard. He won the title of Mr Universe and has been in some of the most iconic movies ever made. He is 6 feet 2 inches tall and weighs over 100 kilograms. His weight comes mostly from muscle, not fat. To say he is intimidating is an understatement. Most people on Earth wouldn't really like to mess with him in person.

A couple of years ago, Arnold was out on holiday with his family. In a relatively empty stretch, another tourist came too close to Arnold. Before anything could happen, Arnold was pushed into a car by a few men and driven away hastily. The men weren't kidnappers, they were his bodyguards. They weren't concerned about teaching the person a lesson. Their first priority was to avoid any kind of situation from happening at all. People imagine being rich and famous as being extremely freeing. It might be, but it does have its downsides. Most very rich and famous people can't just take a walk on the street. They have to be very alert to cameras, the media and safety in general. Warren Buffett used to spend big chunks of his day meeting the people running companies, visiting offices and factories. It allowed him to gain deep insights into what the business was and how good the people running the business were.

In fact fund managers managing a large fund like a mutual fund or hedge fund all follow this practice.

If you look at the Amazon stock between 2000 and 2008, it practically remained flat. But if you knew the kind of moats the company was building around its business, it was only a matter of time before Amazon started producing monopoly-level profits.

So if you believed in the company's ability to execute its plans, you'd buy and wait a couple of years. Some fund managers also knew the same, but most wouldn't be able to hold the stock for eight years. They are answerable to their investors and therefore they mostly like to keep stocks that grow on a regular basis. Think about it, when we as mutual fund investors check out a mutual fund to invest in, we look at its performance over a period of two or three years most commonly. This is also why investors hold many stocks which can go over fifty – too much diversification.

Retail investors can hold a small number of high-performance stocks if they know what they're doing. They are answerable only to themselves – nobody else! Fund managers also struggle to hold too much cash and even when they think stocks aren't attractive, there is pressure on them to invest. But you, unlike them, can just sit with cash till you think the time is right to invest. In fact, if you decide to sell a stock today, you can get the share price that is visible on your dashboard live (more or less).

If a large investor starts selling (or buying), the quantity is such that it starts affecting the price negatively. When they start buying, the price starts rising. When they start selling, the price starts falling. This is why it often takes them weeks to buy or sell a stock. Additionally, what about access to information? Those big guys can surely call up a CEO and ask things. No denying that. But this information gap between professionals and beginners has been bridged to a massive extent in the new internet age where information access is incredibly open to all.

Yes, there are some advantages the big guys have. Still, the point is, yes, being Arnold is cool. But when he looks at a regular person walking on the street without a care, he must feel jealous.

71

Investments Beyond Numbers

BLOOD TESTING IS EXPENSIVE. If you want a cholesterol test done, you need one kind of equipment. If you want a calcium test done, you need another kind of equipment. Each of these pieces of equipment requires a few millilitres of blood. When your doctor wants to get a couple of tests done, the amount of blood required runs into a few millilitres. This is why the medical practitioner who takes blood from your veins collects two or three vials of blood.

Thanks to advancements in medical technology, today, there's one blood test we all can perform easily at home. Blood sugar test. Instead of an injection extracting a few millilitres of blood, the glucometer can tell you fairly accurately the blood sugar levels from just a small drop of blood pricked from a finger. Elizabeth Holmes wanted to change blood testing. She wanted to make it much cheaper, quicker and, above all else, requiring little blood.

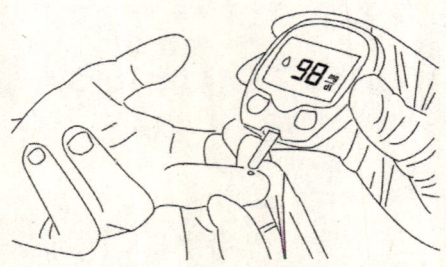

FIGURE 71.1 Glucometer depicting blood sugar levels from a pricked finger

Holmes started working on a new technology in 2004 that promised what others had only dreamt of. Her company, Theranos, with just one drop of blood, wouldn't just be able to deliver sugar test results, it would also be able to tell patients the results of over 200 different tests at a very cheap price than the existing rates.

Bill Gates dropped out of Harvard University to build Microsoft. He became one of the richest people on Earth. Mark Zuckerberg dropped out of Harvard to build Facebook. You don't just drop out of one of the world's most prestigious universities. You have to have something worth leaving college for. Elizabeth Holmes, at the age of nineteen, dropped out of Stanford University in 2004. Stanford is easily one of the top ten universities in the world. She was building Theranos. Some of the greatest names in the technology industry, including Larry Elison, founder of Oracle, invested in Theranos.

By 2010, Theranos had made more progress. Elizabeth Holmes had earned the admiration of the media and the public in general. Many called her the next Steve Jobs. She appeared in the media a couple of times. She was extremely charismatic. Walgreens is a pharmaceutical store chain in America. In 2013, Theranos announced it had tied up with Walgreens to collect samples and conduct tests all over the US.

Theranos had a funding of around $700 million — that's how impressive their pitch was. The company was valued at $9 billion, and Elizabeth owned 50 per cent of that company. She was one of the richest women in the world. But Theranos was taking longer than anticipated in developing its technology. They were struggling to stick to the timeline they had promised. But you need to understand that the problem they were trying to solve was an incredibly difficult one.

One drop of blood, over 200 test results. In 2015, Theranos was given clearance by the FDA for testing the Herpes Simplex 1 virus. First success. Later in 2015, the *Wall Street Journal* published a scathing report on Theranos. They made a bold claim. The claim was that Theranos was using existing older technology to do many tests; that their own technology wasn't being used. To refute these charges, Elizabeth came on TV.

In a famous interview, Jim Cramer asked her to simply put down the rumours about her technology's inaccuracy.[1] He asked her to do so by producing two reports of about 200–300 people showing her technology's results alongside reports from the older existing lab technology. She replied saying that she had already done that. Months moved on, but controversies kept piling up. Elizabeth fought them one at a time. After an inspection of their lab, authorities banned Theranos from conducting further tests due to not meeting certain standards.

Their test labs had to be shut down. But Elizabeth's company was free to make devices to conduct tests at home. She introduced miniLab – a home testing kit. Things went down fast after that. Companies they had partnered with in the past started suing Theranos. The company kept downsizing and reducing staff. It reached a point where finally, in 2018, Elizabeth was charged with fraud. Many media reports say that Theranos's technology didn't exist.[2]

A US court had charged Elizabeth with defrauding investors after a business failure. How did Elizabeth win so much attention for so many years? Investment isn't hard science. Investment requires you to believe someone; someone telling you a dream, someone trying to convince you that they'll achieve their dream. Someone telling you a story. And there's nothing wrong with that. All great achievements start off like that – as dreams.

Every massively successful investment started off as just a dream sold as a great story. Stories of what's possible. Stories of the company's ability to make it all come true. All backed up by skill and years of effort. Theranos was great at storytelling.

72

Just Keep Investing?

With enough time and effort, any wall can be climbed. But still, people build walls around their homes. Why? Because of time and effort — that's the deterrent for many. Very few thieves would want to climb a twenty-foot wall. Some thieves would be willing to climb a six-foot wall. Even more thieves would be willing to climb a four-foot wall.

FIGURE 72.1 A thief trying to climb a six-foot wall

Let's flip this. If you had a shop, you'd want to make it easier for customers to come to your shop. You'd remove barriers for easier entry, make the signboard easy to read, make it look inviting and display what the shop sold. You'd reduce many barriers or sources of friction. A large number of new companies have been built around this technique of reducing the barrier to doing something.

Investing has some pretty giant barriers. One of the most common questions (barrier) among investors pertains to the timing of investment. When should I invest and when should I not? Anyone who has seen the markets closely will tell you that the gyrations in the markets can be quite wild. Are the markets overvalued? Will the markets fall in the next few weeks or months?

There are always investors who will have something to say about it. If you look closely, you'll realise most of these people don't really have a good track record at predicting what the markets will do next. Some people have a very interesting take on the method to solve this particular barrier: just keep buying without worrying about the markets being overvalued or undervalued.

Don't worry about what the interest rates are going to be in the next quarter. Don't worry about anything short-term. Of course, this would also mean that you don't pay too much attention to how your investment performs in the short term. It would also mean that you choose good mutual funds or stocks to invest in. The theory is that if you do this, in the longer run, your investment would have given you good returns.

Often, these returns would be higher than what many investors manage to get by buying and selling at the 'correct' time. Ben Carlson, a portfolio manager and financial writer, tried to demonstrate the merits of this strategy. To show just how effective it can be, he makes things very pessimistic in his example. He talks of a hypothetical investor called Bob who doesn't invest regularly but invests right before every major crash – a very unlucky investor indeed.[1] This investor invests in the

S&P 500 index in 1973 – right before the markets fell by 48 per cent. Then Bob invests in 1987, right before the markets fell by 34 per cent. His next two investments happen right before the crashes of 2000 and 2008. Despite this horrible timing, Bob manages to get around 9 per cent per annum in returns (9 per cent in the US is considered a much better return than in India). So, we see that Bob, despite horrible timing, has managed returns much better than what he'd have gotten from investing in US FDs.

Considering that the alternative to this is the investor not investing in stocks or equity mutual funds, this isn't bad at all. This is assuming the economy of the country itself is in great shape to do well in the long run. If you were investing in the stock markets of countries that have been torn by war or economic turmoil for decades, this strategy (and most other strategies) wouldn't work. In fact, there is one very advanced country where 'just keep buying' wouldn't have worked out – Japan.

Their stock markets have remained pretty flat over decades. How does India hold up? In India, if you invested (by following the 'just keep buying' policy) in an index fund or a good mutual fund or a good collection of stocks, over the last few decades, you'd have made pretty good returns. In fact, the idea behind SIP is to encourage this style of investing. As with all strategies, you need to ask yourself if this one works for you.

Notes

Chapter 4. How 2020 Moved the Markets
1. 'World War 3 Trends on Twitter After US Kills Iran's Top Commander Qassem Soleimani', *Business Today*, 3 January 2020, https://www.businesstoday.in/latest/trends/story/world-war-3-starts-trending-on-twitter-after-us-kills-iran-top-commander-qassem-soleimani-airstrike-242075-2020-01-03
2. Perappadan, B.S., 'India's First Coronavirus Infection Confirmed in Kerala', *The Hindu*, 28 November 2011, https://www.thehindu.com/news/national/indias-first-coronavirus-infection-confirmed-in-kerala/article61638034.ece
3. 'India COVID', Coronavirus Statistics, updated 13 April 2024, https://www.worldometers.info/coronavirus/country/india/
4. Boseley, S., 'Moderna COVID Vaccine has 94 per cent Efficacy, Final Results Confirm', *The Guardian*, 30 November 2020, https://www.theguardian.com/world/2020/nov/30/moderna-covid-vaccine-has-94-efficacy-final-results-confirm

Chapter 6. Investments That Kill
1. Khan, N.A., 'Maruti Reports Lowest Market Share In 8 Years, Tata Motors at 13 Years High', *Economic Times Auto,* 6 April 2022, https://auto.economictimes.indiatimes.com/news/maruti-reports-lowest-market-share-in-8-years-tata-motors-at-13-years-high/90688524

Chapter 7. Investing in the Unknown
1. Waschenfelder, T., 'Circle of Competence: Charlie Munger and Warren Buffett's Greatest Secret', Wealest, https://www.wealest.com/articles/circle-of-competence
2. Ndlovu, N., 'Amazon South Africa Struggles to Find Its Footing', TechCentral, 10 June 2024, https://techcentral.co.za/amazon-south-africa-struggles-footing/246106/

3   Kurian, L.C., 'How Transformation of African Postal Services Help Jumia in Last-Mile', Logistics Update Africa, 14 May 2022, https://www.logupdateafrica.com/e-commerce/how-transformation-of-african-postal-services-help-jumia-in-last-mile-1345405?infinitescroll=1

Chapter 8. Everyone Knows This Brand
1   'Coca-Cola History', The Coca-Cola Company, accessed 10 July 2024, https://www.coca-colacompany.com/company/history#:~:text=Theper cent20Originper cent20ofper cent20Cocaper cent2DCola,newper cent20refreshmentper cent20inper cent20itsper cent20beginning

Chapter 13. When Does a Bubble Pop?
1   Nygaard, C., Ralston, L. and T. Burke, 'AHURI Final Report Series', 328, *Australian Home Ownership: Past Reflections, Future Directions*, 2020, https://www.ahuri.edu.au/sites/default/files/migration/documents/AHURI-Final-Report-328-Australian-home-ownership-past-reflections-future-directions.pdf
2   Lipstein, A., 'What Goes Up', *Harper's* Magazine, June 2024, https://harpers.org/archive/2024/06/what-goes-up-andrew-lipstein-401k-doomsday-index-fund-catastrophe/#:~:text=Asper cent20Keynesper cent20saidper cent3Aper cent20per centE2per cent80per cent9CTheper cent20markets,thanper cent20youper cent-20canper cent20remainper cent20solvent.per centE2per cent80per cent9D&text=Panicper cent20isper cent20theper cent20negativeper cent20image,out)per cent20justper cent20beforeper cent20hisper cent20neighbor

Chapter 14. Thin Line Between Crazy Good and Just Crazy
1   'The New Establishment Summit: Jeff Bezos's interview by Walter Isaacson', *Vanity Fair*, 15 October 2016, *https://www.vanityfair.com/video/watch/the-new-establishment-summit-the-power-of-jeff-bezos*
2   Guzman, Z., 'This Company Will Freeze Your Dead Body for $200,000', *NBC News*, 26 April 2016, https://www.nbcnews.com/tech/innovation/company-will-freeze-your-dead-body-200-000-n562551

Chapter 15. Formula to Hold the Best Performers

1. Bezos, J., 'What They Said in 1999 About Amazon Dot Com', YouTube, posted 27 April 2018, https://www.youtube.com/watch?v=Yv8MrBBuRqI
2. Chodes, A., 'November 8, 1895: Roentgen's Discovery of X-Rays', *APS News,* 1 November 2001, https://www.aps.org/publications/apsnews/200111/history.cfm

Chapter 17. How Many Winners Can There Be?

1. Nurmagomedov, K., 'Khabib Nurmagomedov's Plan for Conor McGregor: "I Want to Break His Face"', YouTube, posted 29 July 2018, https://www.youtube.com/watch?v=KGKpRwX06CI&embeds_referring_euri=https%3A%2F%2Fwww.rt.com%2F&source_ve_path=Mjg2NjY

Chapter 18. Some Winners Keep Winning

1. BBC Team, 'Google Maps Shows Sunken Car Where Missing Man's Body was Found', *BBC,* 13 September 2019, https://www.bbc.com/news/world-us-canada-49677843

Chapter 19. What Changed While You Were Looking at the Stock Price

1. 'Land Reclamation in the Netherlands 1300 vs 2000', *Brilliant Maps,* updated 3 March 2023, https://brilliantmaps.com/netherlands-land-reclamation/
2. https://www.deheus.com/articles/news/the-netherlands-are-almost-the-worlds-largest-exporter-of-agricultural-products-how-did-that-happen

Chapter 20. How One of the Greatest Authors in History Invested His Money

1. Zacks, R., 'The 19th-Century Startups That Cost Mark Twain His Fortune', *Time,* 19 April 2016, https://time.com/4297572/mark-twain-bad-business/

Chapter 21. Where Does Your Advisor Invest

1. 'BRE-X: Inside the $6 Billion Gold Fraud That Shocked the Mining Industry', *Business Insider,* 26 July 2021, https://www.businessinsider.in/stock-market/bre-x-inside-the-6-billion-gold-fraud-that-shocked-the-mining-industry/slidelist/44231985.cms

Chapter 22. The Man Who Gives the Most
1 Singh, R., 'Bhopal: Auto Driver Turns His 3-Wheeler into Free Ambulance, Oxygen On the Go', *Times of India*, 29 April 2021, https://timesofindia.indiatimes.com/city/bhopal/bhopal-auto-driver-turns-his-3-wheeler-into-free-ambulance-oxygen-on-the-go/articleshow/82302489.cms

Chapter 23. Chase the Life and Not the Lifestyle
1 Brandt, A.M., 'Inventing Conflicts of Interest: A History of Tobacco Industry Tactics', *AMJ Public Health,* 102 (1), pp. 63–71, 2012, https://www.ncbi.nlm.nih.gov/pmc/articles/PMC3490543/#:~:text=Althoughper cent20healthper cent20concernsper cent20aboutper cent20smoking,cardiacper cent20diseasesper cent2Cper cent20leadingper cent20toper cent20death
2 'The Marlboro Man Phenomenon: How a Cowboy Redefined Cigarette Marketing in the 1950s', *Brandvertising*, 23 August 2023, https://www.brandvertising.ch/2023/08/marlboro-man/

Chapter 27. If Not This, Then That
1 Crowley, M., Hassan F. and E. Schmitt, 'U.S. Strike in Iraq Kills Qassim Suleimani, Commander of Iranian Forces', *New York Times*, 2 January 2020, https://www.nytimes.com/2020/01/02/world/middleeast/qassem-soleimani-iraq-iran-attack.html
2 Wee, S. and D.G. McNeil Jr, 'From Jan. 2020: China Identifies New Virus Causing Pneumonia Like Illness', *New York Times*, 8 January 2020, https://www.nytimes.com/2020/01/08/health/china-pneumonia-outbreak-virus.html
3 Banker, S., 'Toilet Paper Shortages, Empty Shelves, And Panic Buying: Just How Bad Was Grocery Service In 2020?', *Forbes*, January 2021, https://www.forbes.com/sites/stevebanker/2021/10/01/toilet-paper-shortages-empty-shelves-and-panic-buying-just-how-bad-was-grocery-service-in-2020/

Chapter 28. Which Strategy You Adopt
1 Top Gear, 'Killing a Toyota Part 1', YouTube, posted on 28 September 2010, https://www.youtube.com/watch?v=xnWKz7Cthkk

Chapter 29. Look Left and Right to Cross the Road
1. Jenkins, M., 'Historic Tragedy on Everest, With 13 Sherpas Dead in Avalanche', *National Geographic*, 19 April 2014, https://www.nationalgeographic.com/adventure/article/140418-everest-avalanche-sherpa-killed-mountain
2. 'Is it More Difficult for Vegans to Push Themselves to Physical Extremes?', *BBC*, 23 May 2016, https://www.bbc.com/news/world-36361984

Chapter 34. The Lesser-Known Tulip Tale
1. 'Tulip Mania: Lessons from the World's First Speculative Bubble', Tulip Tools, last updated 26 May 2024, https://www.historytools.org/stories/tulip-mania-lessons-from-the-worlds-first-speculative-bubble

Chapter 37. How Does It Scale?
1. Welch, D., 'An Expert Dismantled a Tesla Model 3. He Found Poor Design and Manufacturing are Squandering Profits', *Los Angeles Times*, 17 October 2018, https://www.latimes.com/business/la-fi-model-3-design-profits-20181017-story.html

Chapter 38. The Monday Unlike Any Other
1. Baker, B., 'Biggest Stock Market Crashes in US History', *Bankrate*, 5 August 2024, https://www.bankrate.com/investing/biggest-stock-market-crashes-in-us-history/#:~:text=Onper cent20Marchper cent2016per cent2Cper cent202020per cent2Cper cent20the,theper cent20sharpestper cent20declinesper cent20inper cent20history

Chapter 39. Bad Decisions and Good Outcomes
1. Aulakh, G., 'China's Xiaomi Launches First Smartphone in India at Rs 14,999', *Economic Times*, updated 9 July 2024, https://economictimes.indiatimes.com/tech/hardware/chinas-xiaomi-launches-first-smartphone-in-india-at-rs-14999/articleshow/38002556.cms?from=mdr

Chapter 47. Simple Is Not Easy
1. Auto Car, 'Tata Nano Driven', YouTube, posted on 23 March 2009, https://www.youtube.com/watch?v=3sZitve3SUw

Chapter 49. The Deepest Recession

1. Kramer, L., 'The Stock Market Crash of 1929 and The Great Depression', *Investopedia*, updated 27 February 2024, https://www.investopedia.com/ask/answers/042115/what-caused-stock-market-crash-1929-preceded-great-depression.asp

Chapter 52. The Advice That Didn't Work in Japan

1. Nakajima, T., Nakamura, M., Yoshioka, K. and W. Antweiler, 'Japan's Economic Growth: Past and Present', *The Japanese Business and Economic System*, edited by Masao Nakamura, 2001, pp. 13–45, Palgrave Macmillan.

Chapter 53. Rules That Stopped Making Sense

1. 'Warren Buffett's Stake in Apple Makes Over $120 Billion This Week', CNBCTV18, updated 5 January 2022, https://www.cnbctv18.com/business/warren-buffetts-stake-in-apple-makes-over-120-billion-this-week-12020572.htm

Chapter 55. Is It a Pond or Is It an Ocean?

1. Moon, D., '"Fish Where the Fish Are" and Other Investing Advice from Warren Buffett's Partner', Knox News, 19 March 2019, https://www.knoxnews.com/story/money/columnists/david-moon/2019/03/19/charlie-munger-investing-advice-daily-journal-corp/3203580002/
2. Lovelace Jr, B., 'Minnesota Confirms First Known U.S. Case of More Contagious Covid Variant Originally Found in Brazil', CNBC, 25 January 2021, https://www.cnbc.com/2021/01/25/minnesota-confirms-first-known-us-case-of-more-contagious-covid-variant-originally-found-in-brazil.html

Chapter 56. All That 2021 Was

1. Banerjea, A., 'Government Nullifies Retro Tax; Introduces Bill to Amend Income Tax Act', *Livemint*, 5 August 2021, https://www.livemint.com/economy/govt-to-amend-income-tax-act-nullify-retro-tax-demands-11628164822039.html
2. Ahmed, A. and M. Kumar, 'Moody's Upgrades Outlook on India to Stable from Negative; Maintains Baa3 Rating', *Reuters*, 5 October 2021, https://www.reuters.com/world/india/moodys-upgrades-outlook-india-stable-negative-maintains-baa3-rating-2021-10-05/

Chapter 57. Why Does Gold Have Value?
1. Hickman, J., 'Look at How Well Gold has Retained its Value from 1000 Years Ago', Schiff Sovereign, 27 September 2018, https://www.schiffsovereign.com/investing/look-at-how-well-gold-has-retained-its-value-from-1000-years-ago-24158/

Chapter 60. Are You Reading Through Your IPO?
1. Santoreneos, A., '$47 Billion to $280 Million: What Went Wrong at WeWork?', *Forbes*, 10 August 2023, https://www.forbes.com.au/news/investing/wework-47-billion-280-million-what-happened/

Chapter 62. When Geniuses Got Together
1. Loomis, C.J., 'A House Built on Sand Meriwether's Once-Mighty Long-Term Capital has All but Crumbled. Why Did Warren Buffett Offer to Buy It?', CNN Money, 26 October 1998, https://money.cnn.com/magazines/fortune/fortune_archive/1998/10/26/250015/index.htm
2. 'Financial Services Report', *Vedder, Price, Kaufman and Kammholz*, 2002, https://www.vedderprice.com/-/media/files/vedder-thinking/publications/2002/06/financial-services-report/files/financial-services-report--summer-2002/fileattachment/financial-services-report_summer-2002.pdf?rev=134de42ade1a4d5cac4252e000051ea6
3. Abbott, R., 'Big Mistakes: John Meriwether and Long-Term Capital Management', *Gurufocus*, 19 June 2019, https://www.gurufocus.com/news/896991/big-mistakes-john-meriwether-and-longterm-capital-management
4. Ibid.

Chapter 64. What Happened in 1991?
1. Soni, M., 'Throwback: When Manmohan Singh Quoted Victor Hugo in Budget Speech', *Hindustan Times*, 18 July 2024, https://www.hindustantimes.com/budget/throwback-when-manmohan-singh-quoted-victor-hugo-in-budget-speech-101721286427173.html

Chapter 66. Markets and Wars
1. Mudgill, A., 'Russian Stocks Nosedive 50 Per Cent as Trading Resumes on Moscow Exchange', *Economic Times*, 24 February 2022, https://economictimes.indiatimes.com/markets/stocks/news/

russian-stocks-nosedive-20-as-trading-resumes-on-moscow-exchange/articleshow/89794446.cms

Chapter 71. Investments Beyond Numbers

1. Holmes, E., 'Theranos CEO: Female Billionaire Changing the World', YouTube, posted on 28 April 2015, https://www.youtube.com/watch?v=FurGeefL-LI
2. Bullez, J., 'How Silicon Valley Got Played by Theranos', *Vox*, 16 July 2018, https://www.vox.com/science-and-health/2018/6/12/17448584/theranos-elizabeth-holmes-bad-blood

Chapter 72. Just Keep Investing?

1. Carlson, B., 'What If You Only Invested at Market Peaks?' *A Wealth of Common Sense*, 25 February 2014, https://awealthofcommonsense.com/2014/02/worlds-worst-market-timer/

About the Author

Groww was born with a mission to make building wealth simple, transparent and delightful. Founded in 2016 by Lalit Keshre, Harsh Jain, Ishan Bansal and Neeraj Singh, Groww seeks to empower Indians in taking control of their wealth by breaking down barriers, whether they are psychological, educational or technical. With an intuitive and user-friendly experience, educational initiatives and a spectrum of financial products, Groww is truly built for a 'growwing' India.

Investments in securities market are subject to market risks, read all the related documents carefully before investing. The securities are quoted as an example and not as a recommendation.

For more information, visit: https://groww.in/p/disclosure